M000221965

Strength Personified

A PERSONAL STORY OF TRAGEDY TO TRIUMPH

Written By: Brittany Cooley
Edited By: Gina Molinari

This book is in memory of and dedicated

to Linda Sue Wilson Cooley.

"...and so it was with peace she found her rest."

(1962-2008)

PREFACE

I can't tell you how many times that I have attempted to write this book. I have typed, backspaced, and deleted dozens of chapters. It's my life story - what could possibly be so difficult about putting it in writing? What makes today different than any other day? Honestly, I'm not sure. I am a firm believer in following my gut, and today my gut says its time. People know me as a happy, bubbly, F-bomb dropping unicorn. The truth is that I've been through a lot and it allows me to have a really light-hearted look on life now. After what I've seen and been through, it's hard to take the petty stuff seriously. So, I want to bring you in and tell you my story. I want to share with you my personal experience with overcoming adversity and beating the odds. Because much like the hunger games, the odds were not in my favor.

So, here it goes...

Overcoming adversity is a skill that I had no choice but to master. Challenges and struggles build our strength and, ultimately, it is the key to our survival. It is my hope that I inspire you to go from simply surviving this life to THRIVING in it and becoming whoever the hell you want to be, despite what's happened or will happen to you. Things don't happen to us. They happen for us. Most importantly, we have the ability to create a beautiful life on the foundation of the pain that we experience.

When you reach the end of this book, I want you to feel inspired to break the mold and make the impossible possible. Because if I can, you can too.

CHAPTER 1

My mother had a childhood illness and was told that she would never have the ability to have children. My conception and birth was truly a miracle for her. I was born on Saturday February 11th, 1989 at 6 pounds, 4 ounces and 22 inches long, healthy with a full head of hair. The circumstances of my birth set a precedent for me to be a survivor. In just 10 years, I would learn just how accurate that was.

My parents divorced in 1995. I spent the weekdays with my mom and weekends with my dad. I had a good life. Two homes, lots of love. I had everything a little girl could ever dream of - besides her parents being together, of course. At the time, I didn't understand why they were separated, but my needs were met so I was content.

My mom and I lived in a big, beautiful five-bedroom home on a hill in Wysox, Pennsylvania. We had a pool. I had two rooms: one for my bedroom and one for my things. In hindsight, I realize this was likely my mom trying to compensate for the difficult move and separation from my father with *stuff*. Things. Toys. Food. Things quickly became an important part of my life that will play out in an incredibly destructive way later. But, for now, Little Brittany was provided for in an incredible way.

Unfortunately, all of that would come to an abrupt end.

At only 6 years old, I don't specifically remember the decline of my mother's mental health. I was too young to understand what was happening. One day we were living in our beautiful home and the next, we were moved in with my grandparents and all of our belongings were put into storage.

It's important that I interrupt this story for a moment to paint you a picture of my mom before you get the wrong idea.

She. Was. Incredible.

For as long as she could be.

Linda Sue Wilson Cooley was the Executive Director of a non-profit organization. Her hair was always perfectly curled, her makeup applied with expert hands. She wore high heels and was the definition of an independent successful woman. In the 90's, that was wildly impressive, particularly as a single mother.

She was beautiful and incredibly talented. She was a fantastic cook, but I remember clearly how she made the most incredible pies. Personally, I was biased to the "ants on a log" and "punkin teeth" that she made for me as snacks. Her voice was heavenly and she loved to dance. Her spirit was the happiest when music was in the air. We sang and danced around our living room together every chance we got. She created magic every night before I went to sleep in the form of the most creative bedtime stories that she would add onto every night.

Holidays were magical and my birthday was always celebrated like a national phenomenon. She sprinkled glitter on my pillow from the Tooth Fairy, shredded carrots for the Easter Bunny, and stayed up late enough to jingle bells outside of my window from Santa's sleigh.

And yet, I remember like it was yesterday finding out that Santa wasn't real. I asked her straight up if he was and she simply looked at me and said, "No." She never lied to me, no matter how much it hurt. Of course, I was devastated and ran to my room and cried for an hour. Then, after much thought, I came back downstairs and made the determination that the Easter Bunny and Tooth Fairy weren't real either. Despite my disappointment, the realization that these characters were made up made me adore her more for being so dedicated to making me feel special every chance she got.

We had two years of this magical life together until it was shattered.

For being such a happy, independent, successful, and all-around amazing woman, she struggled. Silently. The weight of the world was upon her shoulders and no one had any clue. Strong on the outside, dying on the inside. She kept it together for as long as she could until one day... she just couldn't do it anymore.

In November of 1996, my mother suffered from a nervous break-down as the company that she proudly ran for years ran out of funding. I am sure there were many other factors that accumulated and added onto the stress of this. I have heard several stories from others about what caused this breaking point, but I will never know the truth.

This book is a reflection of what I know to be true. I am not writing speculation.

Moving in with my grandparents was an adjustment. I had to switch schools again. But, I easily made friends, so I was eventually content once the adjustment period was over. I missed the beautiful home my mom and I shared together, but the change was fun to me.

To this day, my grandma is my favorite person on this planet. The apple didn't fall far from the tree. The magical creativity, musical talent, and undeniable strength came from my beautiful grandmother. She would leave me "mail" (post-it notes) in my very own mailbox at the top of the stairs. I remember racing home to check it every day after school. We played dress up and dolls. We went for mini hikes in the woods behind her house. We had picnics in the grove with all of my imaginary friends. She created my best childhood memories.

One afternoon in January of 1997, life for me changed forever. Yes, there was the divorce and the subsequent moving around, but this was by far the biggest disruption to my life more than anything that had previously happened. All it took was one event to wreck every chance I had at being normal. One choice made in desperation of my mother's peace that would ruin everything.

For a long time, I fucking hated her for it.

I got off the bus and ran down my grandma's driveway, much like I always did. I walked in the front door and was disappointed when she didn't look too happy to see me. She quietly asked me where my mother was. I responded, "I don't know, Grandma. I just got off the bus." She told me to go to my room and start my homework. I got a snack and did as I was told.

Later that evening, my mom's sister Val came to pick me up. She said I was going to stay with her for a while. I was told that my mom had gotten sick and just needed to get better. For the sake of my little 7-year-old sanity, I went with it. I wrote my mom letters and made her cards while I waited for her to get better.

Aunt Val took incredible care of me. She tucked me in every night and sang our family's childhood prayer with me. Each night I prayed for my mom and aimlessly counted the days until I could see her again.

It wasn't until I was 14 years old, and I had gone through my own hell and back, when I found out what actually happened the night my mom, "got sick."

CHAPTER 2

My mother had been on antidepressants after her break-down. My grandparents were careful to keep them locked in the safe. Due to my mother's instability, they made the decision to monitor and administer her medications.

Shortly after I had gone upstairs to my room and before my aunt retrieved me, my grandmother went to the safe and noticed it was open and the medications were gone. Panic set in. She immediately told my grandfather and called her brother for help.

The EMTs were searching for hours all over the county. Finally, they found my grandmother's car, the car my mother said she borrowed to pick me up from school, pulled over on the side of a dirt road near the house. It was abandoned. The medics searched the woods and found my mother's lifeless body lying face down in the snow. Despite wearing her favorite hunter green wool coat, she was severely frost-bitten and perceived as dead.

She was rushed to the hospital where her clothes were cut off of her. Her stomach was pumped full of charcoal to rid her system of the drugs, but she was deemed a lost cause. She had consumed both of her prescribed medications, amitriptyline and Prozac, in their entirety. Together, these medications are lethal in small doses and should have never been prescribed to her in the first place (*this fact is an entire story of its own, but for the sake of forgiveness and acceptance of the past, I will leave that thought alone right here*).

Despite the odds, my mother survived. She was truly a miracle. She not only lived through the ordeal, but kept all of her fingers and toes as well. The doctors told my grandmother that her daughter would likely lose a hand or a foot, but she never did. Instead, she was sent away to a rehabilitation facility after she physically recovered to work on her mental state after her attempted suicide.

When my mom finally came home, I remember her sleeping a lot. She had a lot of physical ailments and complained of frequent migraines and body aches. We moved back in with my father in an attempt to salvage our family and help her recover. She wasn't Super Mom anymore. She was sickly, weak, and dependent for the first time that I had ever seen. I had a hard time adjusting to this change, and I felt a sense of responsibility for her moving forward. I was afraid to leave her alone because I didn't want her to die. In hindsight, I recognize how sad that was... I was only seven.

I remember my dad packing up the back of his truck to take me camping for the weekend in the woods. I refused to go when it was time to leave because I was afraid to leave her. I knew that broke my poor dad's heart, but I couldn't leave my ailing and fragile Mama Bird.

Eventually, she began to act human again. She wasn't quite back to the way I remembered her, confident and unflappable, but she was better. I had hope and light of Super Mom making a comeback.

On my last day of third grade in June 1998, my mom picked me up from school. I was excited because we were going to the beach for the weekend, just the two of us. It had been years since we had been on a vacation and the beach was our favorite place in the whole world. My grandparents and father felt that it would be good for both of us to go away together. They had been monitoring her progress mentally and physically and collectively decided that it would be okay for us to take the trip.

I didn't know that when she picked me up that day, it would be my last day of school for five years.

Upon hitting the road in my mom's prized possession, her hunter green 1994 Pontiac Bonneville, she revealed to me a few minor changes to our travel plans.

By "minor," I mean pretty major. Nearly a 1,200 mile difference.

Instead of New Jersey, she was changing our destination to Pensacola, Florida. At first I panicked. I cried all the way to the Pennsylvania Turnpike, but I calmed down and realized that this just might be fun. I hadn't been to Florida since we took our trip to Disney World a few years ago. So, I happily rode along in the car with her singing away.

When we arrived in South Carolina, we stopped for the night at a motel. It had been a long day of driving and we had another long day of driving ahead. I demanded that we get a suite because I wanted a King Bed to sleep in. Of course, my mother agreed because she was willing to give me anything to stay calm. It was then and there that I learned how to manipulate her and I realized that I actually had a say in major decisions.

We checked into the room. I ate a snack and got settled.

I remember the stone-faced look she had as if it were yesterday. She grew quiet and said that she had to call Grandma and let her know that we had arrived. She told me not to say anything about where we were, and instead to just tell her that I was okay and I loved her.

Mom got on the phone and dialed Grandma. She lightly told her we had arrived in New Jersey safely and were at her friend Claire's house. This is where we were originally supposed to end up. I hated that Mom was lying. I couldn't help but wonder why. Why was it okay to lie to Grandma? Why was it okay to lie ever? I always got in trouble when I lied. Most importantly, why couldn't we tell Grandma we were going to Florida? What was the big deal? So many thoughts swirled in my head, I felt like I was going to be sick.

I knew from that experience that stability in my life had been depleted and I was about to embark on a journey that was like no other. The cold look of pure deception on my mother's face frightened me. It was as if my mom was no longer there. She handed me the phone, and placed one finger over her mouth to silence me as I said hello and goodnight to my dear grandmother.

She looked like my mom.

She sounded like my mom.

For the most part, she was acting like my mom.

But something was very wrong with her.

Something was off.

She was different.

As I hung up the phone with my grandma, I realized that Mom wasn't Mom anymore. A nasty monster was brewing within her mind. Her mental illness was far from treated. It was just beginning. She was slowly turning into a monster.

Sadly, no one knew.

I finished my snacks and said goodnight. I snuggled up in my huge King Size bed and prayed she knew what the fuck she was doing.

CHAPTER 3

I had my reservations about the lies we told grandma the night before - but I was eight! I had to trust my mom with my life and could only figure she knew what was best. She described the deceit to me as a game to surprise Grandma, Grandpa, and Daddy. Initially, it sounded like a fun game so I played along, not knowing the mental distortion that was just beginning to fester within her mind.

The very first thing that we both wanted to do was find the beach. It was our favorite place in the whole world. It had been the longest car ride ever. I was a great travel companion for my young age, but I was more than ready to get out and BE THERE. I remember asking her how much longer we had to go about 650 times. She was so patient in telling me our estimated time of arrival each time. This was long before GPS and smartphones, so all we had to go off of was the map and printed directions she had found on the computer. I told her to follow the sun and we would find the ocean.

We drove and drove to finally come across beautiful white sand dunes as the sun was slowly sinking over the horizon. I was so excited. I threw off my shoes and ran right to the waves crashing upon Pensacola Beach. Mom barely got the car parked before I took off. I loved the smell of the ocean, the feeling of sand in between my toes, the salt water flowing around my ankles until my feet began to sink into the sand. I had never seen a more beautiful beach in my life. Mom caught up with me and we stood there in awe of God's creation.

As I stood looking out over what was to be our new home, I felt so safe, secure, and happy to be somewhere new with my mama. I remember the look of pure bliss on her face. I was happy that she was happy. I had high hopes for this adventure and the quest we were on to find healing in our lives. A few good months were ahead for us.

Of course, this was before everything was ripped at the seams and all sanctity was lost.

Mom began to talk of a church we were going to attend the next day. She called it the Brownsville Revival. The excitement danced in her eyes as we were to attend the first service there. She spoke of thousands of people that attended this megachurch from all over the world who experienced miracles inside of the church's walls. Mom said she read all about this magnificent place on the internet, and it was the answer to her prayers and all of our problems. She painted a detailed picture of our future that was so beautifully believable. Not just because I was a child, but because she was able to convince everyone she encountered of the beauty of our future.

I was wise for my age, and I studied my mom's behavior and how she interacted with other adults. She was a performer. To this day, I still wonder how she never made it to Hollywood because good grief could the woman put on a show.

We checked into another hotel that wasn't far from the church. We didn't have a master suite like we did in South Carolina, but it wasn't bad for 1998. I was mostly interested in the pool. I loved to swim and I remember spending every waking moment that I was allowed in that pool. Mom always joked that I was born part-fish and called me her little mermaid.

I remember waking up the next morning and Mom encouraging me to get up hastily. "We're going to head over to the church to wait in line!" she said excitedly. But I remember not being terribly excited about waiting in a line all day.

The first time I saw the line, I couldn't believe it. The only thing I can compare it to was the lines for the rides at Disney World. There were hundreds of people lined up with chairs, coolers, and umbrellas all day in the hot Florida sun in front of the church. The doors didn't open until 6:00 PM and before 8 AM the line was quite lengthy. Looking back on it now, I saw striking similarities to a traditional sports tailgate, only with no alcohol. It was comparable to lining up for a concert and desperately wanting to be in the front row. If you didn't wait in line, you wouldn't make it in the main building and would have to sit in the overflow. I had never seen anything like it in my life and, to this day, still haven't. The Brownsville Revival was truly a phenomenon.

Despite the chaos of that line, I don't have any bad memories of waiting in it. That line became the highlight of my week. I was a social little girl and had a very chatty mother. We made so many friends and learned of so many different cultures. That line is where I learned the art of networking and adapting well to my environment. Of course I didn't know that's what I was doing at the time. The only complaint I had was the heat. It was hot as hell, yet I didn't complain much. It was a new experience and an adventure.

I was literally blown away when I walked into the main sanctuary for the first time. It was the most incredible place I had ever been. We walked into a hall so large and extravagant, it took me several minutes to notice that the air conditioning felt so wonderful after waiting so long in the Florida sun. I grew up in a small Wesleyan church with wooden pews and hymnals... I was out of my element in a church of this size. But the building wasn't why people lined the streets for hours in the summer heat. It was what took place during the service.

"The Brownsville Revival (also known as the Pensacola Outpouring) was a widely reported Christian revival within the Pentecostal Movement that began on Father's Day June 18, 1995, at Brownsville Assembly of God in Pensacola, Florida.[1] Characteristics of the Brownsville Revival movement, as with other Christian religious revivals, included acts of repentance by parishioners and a call to holiness, inspired by the manifestation of the Holy Spirit. Some of the occurrences in this revival fit the description of moments of religious ecstasy. More than four million people are reported to have attended the revival meetings from its beginnings in 1995 to around 2000." - Wikipedia

Before I go any further, let's get clear on something: this book isn't about the Brownsville Revival. It is my story. It just so happens that this place of "religious ecstasy" was what pulled me away from my childhood. It became what our lives revolved around for the next four years. I have

held a lot of resentment in my heart towards this place that I am finally laying to rest as I write in this moment. I don't have room in my life for negative emotions anymore, and only operate on an incredibly high frequency of positive vibes.

We attended the Revival five weekday evenings, attended a morning service on Sundays, and attended the prayer meeting on Monday nights to round out our attendance to seven days a week. On five of those days, we were in line waiting for the doors to open. Our lives revolved around the doors opening, the service, and the doors closing. We ate, slept, and breathed this church. I didn't think this was abnormal because I didn't know anything else. After all, what you don't know won't hurt you, right? That was true while it was happening.

However, years later, I learned about all of the things that I missed out on while I waited in lines and attended church seven days a week. I discovered years later that I lead an incredibly difficult life because of it. So yes, it did hurt me. It hurt me for the next decade and a half. I am thankful that it did too, because through my pain I have manifested my purpose. The struggles I was given during five years of endless prayer at this megachurch built who I am today. It is my hope that by reading this, you will rise up and use your pain as your strength too.

After a week living in a hotel, my mom connected with a man who had a "Revival House" right down the road from the church. He told her that he housed people who were coming in from out of town to attend the revival. We went to check it out and decided to make the move over there. It was set up more or less like a group home. It was a nice community house with scripture on the walls and several beds to a room. There was a nice common area and a kitchen. It reminded me of a Christian summer camp I attended the year before; we were just attending another church camp. Except, this one was with my mom all year round. In my childhood ignorance, this seemed pretty cool at the time.

In the meantime, my family was sick with worry. My mom kept telling them that we were extending our vacation because, "we were having the best time!" Then, my grandfather figured out that we weren't in New Jersey at all. Before smartphones, caller ID, Facebook, and Snapchat, it was much harder to find someone who didn't want to be found. I applaud my grandparents for figuring out exactly where my mom and I were by searching through her internet history and stumbling upon my mom's many searches of the Brownsville Revival. Years later, my grandmother admitted that she spent hours running up her long distance phone bill to call the church and asking everyone she could get in touch with if they had seen a woman in her mid-thirties with a nine-year old little girl attending the services.

I think we had been in Pensacola for about two weeks when all of the fun vacation feelings faded quickly into a serious reality check.

I was just a kid who loved her mom. I had high hopes of Super Mom making a full comeback. What better place to do that other than the sunshine state amid palm trees, the ocean, and a cult-like church?

I was an innocent child full of life and love just wanting my mom to get better. Although, I didn't really know what was wrong with her then, I had dreams and visions of her vitality coming back and saw little glimpses of it each day we were there. Surely, she was getting better!

I didn't know what mental illness was. I didn't know it could be more dangerous and deadly than many kinds of physical illnesses. I had no idea that her mind was slowly being overgrown with thick parasitic vines of paranoia and her sense of reality was warping by the minute.

I didn't know that the next decision I made would haunt me for the rest of my life.

I was just a kid.

CHAPTER 3

"LINDA, WHAT THE HELL ARE YOU DOING? HOW COULD TAKE BRITTANY ALL THE WAY HERE AND NOT TELL ANYONE?! YOU DIDN'T EVEN FILL YOUR MEDICATIONS!"

My grandfather had quite the temper. This wasn't the first time I had heard him scream at Mom like this. I hated confrontation and wanted to be as far away from the fight as I could be. I knew she deserved it. *My mom had that same temper. Hell hath no fury like Linda Wilson scorned.* I was in complete panic mode because I knew Mom had been lying to Grandma and Grandpa. She made me lie to them too. I came out of the Revival House's front door and that's when I saw him...

My dad.

Dad rode all the way to Pensacola Florida with my grandfather to bring my mom and I home to Pennsylvania. They brought Mom the medications that she clearly had not been taking. She told me the Lord was going to heal her, so she didn't need them anymore. Quite frankly, I had no idea how long that would take. So far, she had been the happiest I had seen her in a long time, so I thought maybe this crazy church was working.

I was happy to see my dad. I loved him more than anything and wanted nothing more than to have my family together again. I gave him a big hug. He asked me how I was doing. I remember telling him about how much fun Mom and I were having and about the new friends we were making at church.

That's when he said it. "Honey, Grandpa and I came here to bring you home. We don't know if your mom is going to come... but we want you to come home with us."

I remember panicking. Like a full-fledged anxiety attack in my nine-year old body. Complete fear and angst rushed through my veins and I thought I was going to pass out or die. I cried and cried, begging him to let me stay with Mom. I told him he would have to drag me kicking and screaming away from her. Dad told me that he arranged for his friend Bob to come up and build me a treehouse in the woods behind the house like I had wanted. But I just couldn't leave Mom. I knew she needed me.

That day was the second time I broke my dad's heart. I once again chose Mom, over him. A crushed expression washed over his face.

It was the same exact look he had when I backed out of our Daddy-Daughter camping trip.

As a compromise, Mom agreed to take her medications and to come home with me at some point. I can't imagine my Grandpa and Dad would have left if they had thought she wouldn't resurface again for an extended period of time. So, they didn't stay. They drove all that way to turn around and drive all the way back to PA without either of us. A big part of me wished my Dad did drag me away, kicking and screaming. But he just didn't have it in him to break my spirit like I broke his. I'll never forgive myself for that.

After they left, I really did begin to wonder if and when we would go home. In the meantime, I was being cared for and Mom was happy. That's all that really mattered to me. Plus, I fell in love with Florida. The palm trees, the beach, the southern hospitality, and the food. Mom and I frequented Waffle House and Shoney's. They were my favorite. We also discovered Krispy Kreme Doughnuts. There was one right before the bridge to the beach. Every time the sign flashed HOT, we went through the drive thru and got a dozen to devour in one sitting.

I remember the day she asked me what I thought about staying in Florida - like I actually had a say. We were at the beach. Of course, I LOVED the idea. I thought it was THE BEST. But, I was worried about Grandma, Grandpa, and Dad. I thought to myself: "Yikes. Good luck telling them about this. Good. Luck."

CHAPTER 4

We looked at a two-bedroom, two-bathroom apartment on the other side of town from church that was for rent.

It was across from a Circle K, less than a mile away from Burger King, McDonalds, and a Winn-Dixie. The fact that these places were so close was a big deal because we were from the middle of nowhere PA where it took at least 20 minutes to get everywhere.

It had a pool.

A huge playground.

Beautiful landscaping.

Mom loved it and signed the lease that day. I loved it too. I could swim as often as I wanted all year round. We weren't that far away from church, and only about 20 minutes from the beach. It was perfect. I thought we were finally getting somewhere. I felt like I was finally getting my mom back as we created some stability for ourselves.

She sang and danced around. She was vibrant and full of life again. She was happy. Therefore, so was I. All I ever wanted was for her to be happy and healthy again. I was blind to the fact that her mental health was in fact declining at a rapid rate. I was blind to her behavior being slightly abnormal.

I remember the day she called Grandma and Dad and told them she got an apartment and we weren't, in fact, returning to PA. I remember hiding in my room. I felt like I was going to throw up. It was right before we were about to walk out the door for an evening church service.

I remember her handing the phone to me after she got done speaking with each of them, arguing, because they wanted to hear that I was okay. That same cold, stone look that I saw on her face in the hotel in South Carolina washed over it. It was as if something evil possessed her. I was frightened, so I put on my happiest voice and told my Grandma that I really loved the apartment, that I wanted to stay, and that Mom was good. I said the same to my Dad. I heard his heart break over the phone. That was the third time I broke his heart. I was thankful that it wasn't in person, so I didn't have to see that look on his face, though I could see it clearly in my head as he spoke anyway. I wasn't lying about anything I said to them, but I had a strange feeling about that look on my Mom's face. But I was a kid, and the worry left me as quick as it came.

How was I to know I shouldn't trust my own mother?

After I hung up, I felt a wave of relief because the truth was out, and we could live our lives happily together in a new adventure. The truth will always set you free.

Day in and day out, our lives revolved around Brownsville. Mom insisted we attend every service. I learned to make the best of it and decided that if you can't beat them, you have to join them. My survival skills were being built little by little. At the time, I had no idea just how important they would be.

We eventually didn't have to wait in line anymore and were saved seats in the main sanctuary. I remember, Mom often made me dress up for church. Dressing up was seriously the worst. I was only ever happy in shorts and t-shirts. Mom always said, "Cleanliness is next to godliness, Brittany," when I complained. I never understood what that had to do with clothing, but she was the boss. At least she was at that time. This was before our roles were reversed.

I got involved with Kingdom Kids, the church program for youth. I would get so excited for Wednesday nights. I enjoyed all of the programs. The music and the messages were so entertaining. The kids' pastor was incredible. I made so many friends. I never wanted to leave. I was always disappointed when it was over.

My favorite part of church period became worship. The aisles and altar were flooded with metallic flags that shimmered and ribbon dancers with tambourines. Everyone would sing and dance. It was magical to be a part of and mesmerizing to watch.

The worship team and pastors were like celebrities. I personally idolized them all. Lindell Cooley was the worship leader. I thought it was cool because we had the same last name and everyone thought we were related. Charity would sing, "Come Running" at the end when the Evangelist, Steve Hill, would end his powerful messages. Then he would ask anyone who wanted to be "saved" to come and kneel at the altar. The altar was always flooded with hundreds of people crying and seeking God's forgiveness.

Mom had become really good friends with the man who operated The Revival House where we first stayed when we arrived in Pensacola. He said that he needed help because so many people were coming to the church. He needed an overflow for people to stay when his house got full. So the room in our new apartment that was supposed to be mine was quickly turned into the Revival overflow. Two bunk beds replaced my one twin bed and we hosted guests from all over the world.

Hans George and Weibke were my favorite. Their German accents and culture were fascinating to me. Years later, when I had the choice to study Spanish or German, I chose to study the German language because of them.

I was completely fascinated by all of our guests, especially the internationals. I dreamed of going overseas and traveling to their countries. I dreamed of what their culture was like and how I would fit in there. I asked so many questions that it most likely drove them crazy. I told them all that someday, when I was old enough, I would visit them and they could bring all of their stories to life. I fell ill to the travel bug at nine years old.

It was quite an eventful summer. I left my last day of third grade at Camptown Elementary School for, "a quick beach trip to New Jersey" and ended up in Pensacola, Florida adapting to a brand new life - away from everything and everyone I had ever known. My future gleamed with brightness and the tunnel was lit up in such a magnificent way. Sure, I missed my Grandparents, Dad, and all my friends from school, but my heart was with my Mom. This was truly an adventure. Mom always said, "It's just you and me, kid. You and me against the world."

CHAPTER 5

The summer faded without a change in seasons. It didn't feel like back-to-school time. I hadn't really thought about school at all. I didn't dislike school, but I did have a huge fear of being, the new kid. No kid ever wants to be the new kid. It was then that I missed my tiny elementary school and friends more than ever. I wished I could bring that school and all my friends to Florida. Yet, I still had no true desire to return home.

Mom networked with other moms of the kids at church and found their homeschooling program, Brownsville Kids. Many of the church kids were homeschooled by their parents because they feared the public school system wasn't a safe, Christ-like environment. The homeschool program offered art classes and extracurriculars like chorus for social interaction. Mom was all about homeschooling me and having me even more engrossed in the church. *As if being there 6-7 days a week wasn't enough already.* Ultimately, I loved the idea of homeschool because then my fear of being the new kid wouldn't have to be a reality.

There was a big, fancy private Christian school called Pensacola Christian Academy. A lot of the wealthy church members' children went there. Mom and I went to tour it and I was in awe. I wanted to go there so badly, but Mom couldn't afford the tuition. She said, "Maybe next year, babe!" I was okay with that because I thought being homeschooled meant I could sleep in. I loved to sleep. *I swear I was born with a repulsion to mornings.*

Mom figured out what she had to do legally to homeschool me in the state of Florida. She went and purchased the fourth grade curriculum and I was officially a fourth grader. Sort of.

I loved chorus and art class. They were my favorite. Mrs. Gladstone was the chorus teacher and I absolutely adored her. I wanted to be her when I grew up. She had the most beautiful voice, aside from my Mom. I made friends within our little district of homeschooled church kids and looked forward to every chance I had at interacting with them. Eventually, Mom would pull me from those programs because they were an extra expense she couldn't afford to pay for anymore. She said she had to give more money to God, and we had to make sacrifices in order to please Him.

When it comes to school, I honestly don't remember learning much or spending any significant amount of time on actual lessons. Mom tried to teach me some things and I did some work in the books, but I wasn't the most motivated nine-year old. I certainly wasn't going to crack open a math book on my own without a severe prompt or threat. I was the kid that loved reading, gym class, and recess. Academics were for the birds. I hated math, I hated homework, and I hated doing anything that I didn't want to do. I desperately needed structure, and there just wasn't any.

Mom's priorities began to shift and her mental health began to rapidly decline. I didn't know it at the time, but looking back almost 20 years later with six years of adult mental health social work experience under my belt, it's crystal clear.

I remember that I was on my own a lot. I went to the pool and played on the playground. I explored the apartment complex and the housing development that was connected to ours. It was full of brand new beautiful homes. I would daydream about what it would be like to live in a big, brand new home like those.

I created my own version of reality so I didn't die of boredom. I spent a majority of my day outside. I made lots of friends who lived in the complex and began to play with them regularly. They all went to school during the week, so I became very good at keeping myself company. I became incredibly good at being alone.

I began to sneak into the youth service that was for ages 14-18. I felt as though I was outgrowing Kingdom Kids, even though I was within the age range for it. I loved being around teenagers. I couldn't wait to be one so I could fit in better there.

That is when I met Isaiah.

Isaiah was my first real crush. *(I had my first kiss under a slide at my babysitter's house when I was 6. It was gross and my repulsion to boys grew after that day. We had seen a boy and a girl kissing in a movie and wanted to see what the big deal was. Turns out, it wasn't. I never wanted to kiss another boy ever again. When I was 8, my next kiss almost happened one day during recess. I cornered one of my class-mates in the jungle gym made of tires and asked him to kiss me. He ran out the other side. He was supposedly my boyfriend too. My dom-inance was slightly intimidating even at age 8.)*

He was the tall, blonde hair, blue-eyed, hysterical personality that everyone loved and loved to be around. His energy lit up the entire sanctuary and I could always spot him from rows and rows away. I don't think I actually spoke to him for about a year. He was a big part of my sneaking into Youth Group. I admired the way he danced and worshiped and prayed. He was sincere. Genuine. Anyone that came in contact with him could feel the goodness within his soul. He was kind to everyone.

I had never been around anyone like him and I wanted to be in his inner circle. I remember the first day he talked to me. I nearly passed out. I felt as I did the time I met Aladdin at Disney World. The char-acter knelt down, touched my cheek and said, "Hi, sweetie, how are you?" Who knows what I said or did, but I am confident that it was embarrassing. I had never felt so strange. Every time I saw Isaiah I felt sick, but in a good way. If that makes any sense at all.

That majestic teenage dream boy that I drooled over for four years - and still have a soft spot in my heart for today - is what grounded me when things got bad with Mom. His friendship is what gave me relief from what was happening around me. So, I am incredibly thankful for the friendship that Isaiah gave me by allowing me into his inner circle of friends. I truly believe I wouldn't have survived without him and his positivity. He was my light when dark things happened in my life.

Our first year in Pensacola was truly beautiful. We made many memories, enjoyed Florida life, and each other. That was the last happy year we had together. As bizarre and unhealthy as our church schedule and my lack of schooling were, I cherish it with all my heart.

We were happy.

We were together.

We were safe.

It was the last happy year we that we had together in this lifetime.

CHAPTER 6

I remember Mom talking about running out of money. A lot. She wasn't talking to me, but herself loudly. Maybe she didn't think I heard, or maybe she thought I didn't understand. But I knew things were bad. I remember her angrily on the phone with someone and learning that her disability was going to run out. I remember her abnormally talking to herself, speaking in tongues, and rebuking the devil. Her face was as red as a cherry tomato.

Later on, I discovered that she received about $2,000 per month in disability. That was our income. That was more than enough to live on in the 1990's. The problem was that she had to go to a doctor annually to have it renewed and be declared medically or mentally unable to work. Her illness was worsening, and she claimed that medical doctors were of the devil. She believed that God had spoken to her and instructed her not to make a doctor's appointment because they did the devil's work. She firmly believed, and stated multiple times, that it was against God's will for either of us to go to the doctor. She would say that God would take care of us no matter what.

Because of her refusal to get a signed letter from a physician to approve her disability benefits moving forward, our funding source was cut off. We ran on savings for as long as we could until that eventually ran dry too.

I didn't know what it was like to struggle up until this point in my life. Whatever I needed or wanted I always had or received. There was always food when I was hungry; there were always clothes when I needed them. There was always a shower to bathe in and a bed to sleep in. To be perfectly honest, I had been spoiled rotten even throughout my mother's breakdown. I never went without. I didn't know or understand the word scarcity. I had never been told "no."

She burned through her savings.

She cashed in her retirement pre-maturely.

$26,000.

It was all gone in less than six months.

I know she gave a lot of it to the church because it was, "God's instruction" to do so. But, she also bought lots of bibles and expensive journals for her ministry and...who knows what else. A huge part of me doesn't want to know.

I really started to notice that there was something wrong with Mom when she began to let herself go. She wouldn't shower regularly anymore. She wouldn't wash clothes for weeks. She began to smell. She took a majority of my clothes and things I had loved and bagged them up and threw them away. I cried myself to sleep most nights during this time because I didn't understand why she was getting rid of everything I had. She would buy me a brand new outfit and then the very next day cut it up and throw it away saying the devil was inside of it.

She emptied the apartment. I was sleeping on an air mattress in the living room on the floor.

She became incredibly paranoid. It would come out of nowhere. She would randomly say, "We need to leave" and instruct me to follow her out the door. We would get in the car and go. Sometimes we would go to church or another random location and sit in the parking lot. Sometimes we would go to the beach or the Natural Oaks Park. Sometimes we would be sitting in church and she would instruct me to follow behind her in a few minutes because "they" would see us together and kill us both.

Later on, I learned how to use this in my favor. In our favor. I began to realize that if I couldn't beat her, I had to join her. I said what I needed to say to get her where she needed to go. It sounds a lot like manipulation, but it was really for our own survival.

We ate like queens right after she cashed in her retirement. I remember going to fancy seafood restaurants in Destin and she would drop $200 on a meal for just two of us. I wished that I could go back and budget that out in dollar menu meals for years after. It was nice while it lasted. But, it certainly didn't last.

When money finally ran low, we began to eat fast food for every meal. This was the beginning of my nasty eating disorder and incredibly unhealthy relationship with food. I knew Mom was getting worse. I didn't understand mental illness, but I knew there were screws loose. I knew that she was not behaving like other children's mothers. I was very observant and she was just... off.

So, I ate.

The only thing that made me feel better about her condition and the instability we were facing was food. I was always safe if I had food. I felt a sense of comfort and love when I ate. It was way more than hunger that it satisfied. It was what I looked forward to everyday. It is how I got through the days. I ate my feelings. Food was always there for me.

Until it wasn't.

That is when I tapped into my newly-honed manipulation skills and put them to good use. Think what you want, but this is what kept us fed and under the radar for as long as possible. This was the beginning of the transition of power from my mother, to me.

I was the boss. I called the shots. It was on me. I gladly took on the role as caretaker, leader, "Mother", because I didn't see another option. She needed me more than ever. I was the only person who understood her mind and began to learn how to I control it. I also realized that this worked on other people.

I began to hang out with my friends from the complex more at their apartments, purposely around meal times. They would always offer me a plate.

No matter how bad things got, there was one thing I could never stand to do: beg. I was no beggar. Nor would I resort to it. I knew there were better ways.

At my friend's houses, I would eat half my meal and take the other half back home to my mom. Some days I would eat more than half and feel so guilty about it. This is how we lived for a few months once we ran out of money.

Then one day there was a giant neon green sign placed on the outside of our door. We were served eviction papers and had 30 days to vacate. We had nowhere to go.

Mom had burned many bridges in the church when she started going downhill mentally and emotionally, so there weren't a lot of options for us. I had already been dodging caseworkers left and right. We had countless reports filed for neglect. There was an investigative case in the making. I remember telling caseworkers looking for a "Brittany" that my name was Stephanie and Brittany lived upstairs with her mom. I told the poor caseworker that I would let her know someone was looking for her, and even took her card. That happened several times.

Looking back years later and having briefly worked in child protective services, I feel terrible about all of the paperwork we caused them. Back then, it was all handwritten too. Jeesh, they must have hated me.

We still went to church, and for that I was thankful. Church was the only time I had some relief. I would leave Mom in the main sanctuary and go find Isaiah and his group of friends. I couldn't leave her for too long, but long enough to have somewhat of a break from the insanity. The youth group truly gave me some peace and sense of normalcy. It was a time I got to interact with sound-minded individuals.

I prayed every service that some kind of miracle would happen, because Lord, we needed it. I wasn't sure how much longer we were going to make it.

I loved my friends. I loved them so much for just being my friend. I found so much value in them, just by having someone to sit next to that wasn't her.

I was growing tired of Mom's bullshit. I finally began to do whatever I could to be away from her as much as possible. I know that sounds terrible, but I really started to resent the woman. She was robbing me of my life, and I knew it.

But, I also knew that it was my duty to make sure she lived. I felt as though it was my calling as her protector. She always came first. Even when I absolutely hated her, she always came first.

I created a fantasy that I lived in for a little while each day, just to survive. I would dream about going to Pensacola Christian Academy and wearing a uniform. Sometimes, I thought I was going crazy. I would see other mothers and daughters in public and wonder what it was like.

What was it like to have a stable home environment and go to school?

I had forgotten.

What was it like to have cabinets full of food?

I had forgotten.

What was it like to be a kid?

I had completely forgotten.

I was just trying to make it through each day. I had no long term plan, but every night I laid down on my deflating air mattress in that living room thankful we made it another day.

At the time of our eviction, I had two ferrets, Flower and Fayline. I had a bunny named Snuggles. My large rodents were everything to me. I loved them and cared for them like they were my children. I always made sure they were fed. Even if I was hungry. I begged Mom for pets when she cashed in her retirement, so she agreed. But now that we had nowhere to go, I knew I had to give them up.

The day I gave up my ferrets and Snuggles, I cried harder than I ever had. That broke my heart more than starving or being evicted. I felt a kind of sorrow and loss I had never felt before. I was bitter and resentful. I borderline hated my mother at this point. I didn't understand why she couldn't just go get a job like normal moms did. She kept saying God was going to provide for us, but he never did. We were hungry, broke, and soon to be homeless. I had lost everything. All I had left was five or six pieces of clothing.

But I still stayed.

When the Escambia County Sheriff's Department showed up with that neon green sign to plaster on our door to serve us with official eviction papers, shit became very real. I asked Mom if she had a plan, constantly. She always answered, "The Lord will provide for us." I was incredibly skeptical of her view on God and his plan to take care of us, but I was hoping with everything in my being that she was right.

I spent a lot of time wishing that she wasn't crazy. I kept waiting for what she said was going to happen to actually happen and prove me wrong. In fact, I remember praying for that. A lot.

The next thirty days were the worst. I felt like we were on death row, only instead of walking the green mile, the Sheriff and the apartment complex manager escorted us out of the only home we had and onto the street.

Mom threw away everything we had aside from a few outfits for each of us and what would fit in the trunk of our car. We left our apartment at Carriage Hills at 6AM on the last possible day. I'm glad Mom didn't wait for the Sheriff escort to avoid some of the drama that could have occurred. Our first destination was down the road to the McDonald's. Mom went inside to get a coffee and I fell asleep in the backseat. That was the first of many sleeps I would have inside of our Bonneville.

CHAPTER 7

At this point, if there was anything I was good at, it was adapting to my environment. I quickly got used to homeless life just like I had gotten used to everything else that had come along. We would sleep at abandoned rest areas at night and during the day we would sit at bookstores. I considered us upper-class homeless people because we had a car and a $50 per week income via my father's child support check. I dreaded the days that would be cut off because that was our sole source of survival. Thankfully, I was in charge of the money.

We had a post office box where we received our mail. Grandma would write letters and include money sometimes. That was the best! We got a room once per month at Motel 6 so we could shower and sleep in a real bed. That's what I looked forward to the most: a hot shower and a bed.

We ate off the dollar menu mostly. Towards the end of the week was harder. Sometimes Mom and I would have to split a four-piece chicken nugget and that would be it for the day. I remember pocketing ketchup packets to eat when I got hungry. I never shared them with Mom and I always felt so guilty for that. We would try to hold off on eating until 3:00 PM so we wouldn't be starving all night. It was so hard to sleep when you were starving. But sleep was important, especially for life on the streets.

The days seemed to drag on forever until I began to utilize the resources I had at my fingertips - books. We spent a lot of time at Barnes and Noble and Books-A-Million bookstores. I decided to read to pass time. It was probably the best thing I could have ever done, especially being out of school for so long.

I read everything from the entire *Goosebumps* collection to *Anne of Green Gable* to an entire book on Monet because I loved his paintings. I read about politics and Elvis Presley. I read about the female reproductive system which is where I learned about menstruation and puberty (thank God for that). I remember the day I got my period for the first time; I immediately knew what to do. If I hadn't read that book, I surely wouldn't have.

Being a pre-pubescent homeless girl totally sucked. No money for pain reliever or feminine products meant suffering through the awful cramps while being creative. I can clearly remember one instance when I was lying down in the front seat of the car. Mom and I had been parked near a playground/rest area that day. I had the seat reclined back as far as it would go. I literally wished death upon myself because the bleeding and pain was so bad. I had wads of toilet paper stuffed in my underwear, lined with newspaper to prevent ruining the only pair I had. That was reality. The pain was so bad that I nearly blacked out. I fell asleep and woke up so grateful that the pain was gone.

It was kind of like an adventure. An adventure of survival. I was incredibly grateful for every meal I had, every hour of sleep I got, and especially the unexpected blessings we would receive. Sometimes the lady in the cafe at the bookstore would "accidentally" make an extra mango smoothie or break a scone. I remember one day I found an entire unopened bag of funions - like, a BIG bag - and I ate them all in minutes. Another time, a girl from church youth group brought us a big family-sized meal from Wendy's and dropped it off to us. Sometimes we would splurge our money and go to a buffet and eat until we couldn't eat anymore. We didn't know when we could eat again, so we made it count.

Thinking back, I wonder how we didn't get caught sooner. Sure, child protective services had an open investigation, but my family had no idea what was going on or where we were. We stayed under the radar for a long time.

We attended church less frequently because of gas and the inability to drive back and forth. When we had the opportunity to go, it was a treat. I liked going to church after we had a shower so I didn't smell around my friends. I always looked forward to seeing Isaiah. Although I knew I wasn't that pretty and I didn't have fancy clothes (and my mom was pretty crazy), he never treated me any different than the pretty, cleaner girls in our circle. I was so thankful for that.

Even with church still an important part of our lives, it's as if everything crumbled at once. Everything was fine, until it wasn't.

She had taken everything from me. All of my things, my family, my peace of mind, my sense of security, and every last ounce of stability I had. She wiped away any sense of normalcy I had and essentially brainwashed me into believing that everything was totally okay. Things were bad, but I remained faithful to her. I swore on my life I would never leave her side. I knew she needed me. I knew she would never make it alone. I knew that I was the only person on this earth who could make sense of her disturbed and infected mind. So, when I found a quarter on the ground to make a call to my father on the payphone outside of the old Winn-Dixie, I didn't. I knew I was sacrificing the last chance I had at being rescued. Instead, I faithfully took the quarter back to the car. That day, when mom woke up from her nap, I shared it with her in excitement. "Hey, look what I found! Maybe we can find two more quarters somewhere and get something in the vending machine to split for dinner!" She was so happy. A big smile spread across her face and she said what she always did: that God was providing for us. I couldn't help but wish that He could be doing just a little bit more.

Mom's paranoia got worse. She made up names of imaginary characters and began to believe that the evangelist and pastor were conspiring against her. I had to learn how to talk to her to make her do what she needed to do. I said whatever I had to say to get her to where she had to go.

For a while, it was all trial and error. Some things worked, others didn't. I learned quickly because our cover would be blown if she didn't get her act together. Once child protective services got their hands on me that would be it. We would be separated forever and she would likely never get me back. I knew that.

We were noticed a few times in the bookstores and questioned by nosey people. I concocted a good story about how my mom was a minister and writing sermons while I was homeschooling and we, "just spent a lot of time here so she could study for her bible school exams." That wasn't true at all, but it was what she wished was true.

I began to wash my hair in the Barnes and Noble bathroom sink in the handicapped stall. Appearance was everything. We couldn't look dirty if we wanted to stay on our own. I also took some of our weekly food money and demanded we wash a load of laundry once a month. We barely had 3 outfits a piece so it wasn't hard to fit all that into one load and we could air dry most of it so we didn't have to spend extra money on the dryer.

Are you still with me? Because the story hasn't truly begun yet.

I am not sure how any of what came next was able to transpire because it was as if the courts favored my mother bringing me back to the depths of hell and they couldn't realize she was crazy.

In 2001, we returned to Pennsylvania for a visit. Mom swore that we were just home temporarily. I don't remember that much about these few months because we returned to Florida as seemingly quickly as we arrived. Unfortunately, this time we returned for a visit with conditions worse than when we had left.

I don't remember how we got back to Pennsylvania. I don't remember where I stayed primarily.

This is what I do remember: I was briefly enrolled in a small private Christian school. It was seventh grade and I was severely behind, especially in math.

I remember being at my Grandma Cooley's house on 9/11. I ran into the kitchen when the news was announced on TV. I remember disliking Dad's new girlfriend. I remember being thankful for the meals and the bed and the showers, but for some reason I already knew that they wouldn't last. Mom was hell bent on returning "home" to Florida and taking me with her. I know my family did everything in their power, but at the end of the day, my mom was a con artist and walked her ass right out of that courtroom with what she wanted: an agreement and a way to get back to Florida with me.

At the time, I didn't know what went on behind the scenes. I knew it was heavy, but I was sheltered from most of it. I think my family tried to keep me out of it as much as they possibly could because they thought I was just a kid and didn't need to hear the gory details of things like this. In all actuality, they had no idea what I had been dealing with and court was the *least* of my hardships under Mom's care.

I knew it was going to happen because I knew my mother. I was nearing the age of 13. I had half of a year of seventh grade under my belt, the only type of formal schooling I had since I was nine. I knew we had nowhere to live, no food to eat, and a whole lot of hell to endure. But, I agreed to go back to Florida with her. I agreed because I knew that I couldn't leave her. She wouldn't make it.

Even as a pre-teen, I had known that she couldn't survive in the mental state she was in without me. It's amazing, really. She was a stickler for getting what she wanted when we arrived, but when left to her own devices, she could barely take care of herself. She was an actress playing a role to get where she wanted to go. I knew, and yet I had to play along too, because I honestly had become afraid of her.

None of it made me love her any less, though. I accepted her for who she was.

Years later, I found the court documentation that allowed my mother to return to Florida on the conditions that she sought medical care and provided a home for me along with schooling. She was also supposed to allow me to return to Pennsylvania for the summers to spend with my father.

(As I write this, I am looking at that agreement right now. There are times where I think, maybe that was all a movie I watched. But these court documents date-stamped from 2001 don't lie. Having all of this paperwork in front of me verifies that none of this is made up and it all actually happened. It wasn't some twisted dream.)

I'm sure you're thinking, "What kind of judge orders this?!" Well, my friends, you have underestimated the power of Linda Cooley and her ability to lie like a pro. I can only imagine the horror my family must have felt when the judge made the decision. My aunt and father were worried to death. For some reason, I wasn't. Mom and I couldn't be separated. Where she went, I went. I could handle her. Plus, Pennsylvania was cold.

Mom would never hurt me or let anyone hurt me, right?

I thought so.

I thought wrong.

I underestimated her illness. I would have never returned to Florida had I known the nightmare that awaited me. She turned on me and left reality far behind her. I broke my Dad's heart for the fourth time when I left again, and that look on his face haunted me. It wouldn't be nearly as devastating as the next time in 2012 but, we have a long way to go before we get there.

If the past three years didn't fuck me up bad enough, this next chapter of life with her surely did. I learned to embrace self-harm and idealized suicide as comfort. I was going to have my innocence ripped away from me and wish I was dead.

CHAPTER 8

When we returned to Florida, we stayed at the Revival House for a little bit with that nice man who had helped us before. But, due to Mom's antics, our warm welcome and invitation to stay was quickly revoked. Her behavior became unbearable to most everyone we encountered. I knew that meant her illness was worsening. I often wished she would just wake up one day and be normal. But, that never happened.

Mom got a job working for a paraplegic woman, we will call her Darcy. Darcy had us move in to her spare bedroom as Mom agreed to care for her as a kind of home health aide. Mom had to bathe her, dress her, and give her enemas. She had to help Darcy brush her teeth and feed her every meal. It was very demanding work that required a lot of Mom's time and felt very limiting to escape for any time for ourselves.

Mom's illness worsened during this time. Darcy was a complete nightmare. She had Mom up at all hours of the night and beckoned her every chance she got. Mom and Darcy would get into fights like you wouldn't believe. There were times I almost believed this was punishment for Mom's lying and deceitful behavior. Secretly, I was enjoying her having to actually work and be treated this way. I just wish I hadn't been in the middle of it.

I remember going for walks everyday with my Walkman. It was the one thing that I would never let Mom touch or sell because it was my saving grace. Music was the key to my sanity and the *sole* reason I made it for as long as I did. My Dad had bought it for me when I was home in Pennsylvania for that short period of time in 2001.

I listened to Mary J. Blige and Britney Spears. I had one of those music compilation albums - Now That's What I Call Music: Volume 11, if I recall correctly. I would go for a walk everyday with my headphones around Darcy's neighborhood and pretend I was someone else. I would walk to the beat of the music and pretend I was in a music video or someone that wasn't me. Anyone.

Whenever life became too unbearable in reality, I would just tune out the world and go to my made-up happy place. I walked miles and miles. Some days, I would feel better after only a few songs, around 15-20 minutes. Others, I would walk for hours.

One day, I was stopped by a policeman. He asked why I wasn't in school. In my head I replied, *"Oh, my mom is crazy and I haven't been in more than three months of school for nearly four years, and I'm starving."* But, of course, I didn't say that to him. The scary part about this encounter was that I felt like I was turning into my mother. I wanted to be nothing like who she was these days. She was a liar. But, that's exactly what I became. I justified my lies because I had to keep us safe - to keep us together. We were almost split up before. That couldn't happen again.

Instead of the truth, I told the officer a different version of the same bullshit story that I told every caseworker or concerned citizen that ever tried to pry into my life. I said I was homeschooled and on a 15-minute break for the day. I was 13, but actually said I was 15. My name was Bethany and my mom was a caretaker for a disabled woman in the neighborhood. He bought every word, told me to be careful, and sent me on my merry way. I turned up my Walkman, which was coincidentally playing "No More Drama" by Mary J. Blige, and continued my walk in my pretend life until I had to return to my grave reality.

This was when I began to become bitter. I was angry when I saw normal kids getting off the school bus and greeting their parents. Why couldn't my mom get her shit together? Why couldn't we have our own home? Why couldn't she just snap out of her weirdness, lies, and paranoia and just be my mom again? I began to resent her, but I still stayed by her side because I knew she needed me. Every day it became more and more apparent that that was never going to change.

I had my way out, and I didn't take it. I had my chance to stay with my dad in a stable home with family and regular meals, and I left. I left and followed Mom because - despite all the harm she caused for both of us - my commitment to this woman was stronger than my need for stability. I was willing to sacrifice to be with her in hopes she would snap the hell out of it. I let Mom lie to everyone, including my family and the court, to come right back to hell with her.

We didn't last long at Darcy's house. She couldn't stand my mom for more than a few months. So, we were back on the streets living in our car and eating out of garbage cans. We were again showering in Barnes and Noble bathrooms, stealing potted meat and 88-cent rolls from Wal-Mart just to survive. I always felt bad stealing. But my theory was, if it was food and that cost less than $1, it was okay.

We were hungry. Hungrier than ever. Mom would call and check in with Grandma from time to time to keep them away. I would get on the phone and lie about how things were.

I was angry, dirty, hungry, and lonely. I couldn't tell anyone what life was really like. Even when we went to church, my friends were always happy to see me. I did my best to try to fit in and pretend like my life wasn't as bad as it was. Youth group helped with that, but it didn't last forever. The service would end, and everyone would go home with their parents. I would go find Mom in the parking lot sitting in the car, and we would drive to another parking lot to sleep.

I was so over it.

Mom was above going to the soup kitchen, but there was a time when I begged because I was that hungry. I just wanted to sit down and eat a hot meal with other people who were like us. I wanted to feel anything but hungry. I concocted a ridiculous story to get Mom to go. I told her that I believed God told me we had to go there. This wasn't the first time that I had said something like that to get what

I wanted, nor would it be the last. Often times it would amaze me that Mom couldn't see through my lies. She was smart, but maybe I was smarter.

I felt guilty for lying in the name of the Lord. I had learned at church for years that it was an unforgivable sin. But, I did what I had to do. To keep us safe. To keep us fed. To keep us from being separated.

We were lucky that we had the opportunity to come back to Florida together. I was hesitant to go back to a life of structure. I didn't want to go to school and have rules. I was the boss for a long time. I wanted to keep it that way. I became comforted in the fact that we were scavengers and scraped by each day. I didn't want that to be jeopardized, so I lied.

I became *almost* as good as Mom at lying. It scared me sometimes, because I wanted to be nothing like her. She was a monster. But, I understood that she was a sick monster that somewhere, deep inside, held my Super Mom captive. The Mom that used to dance around to R.E.M. in our beautiful five-bedroom home just five years ago… I knew she was still in there somewhere. I had held on to that all these years.

Until she fed me to the wolves.

CHAPTER 9

"Brittany, this is God's will and you are to serve him in this way. I have to write a sermon for my church. My disciples need their shepherd. The Lord is calling me to go up on the mountain with him. I have to be alone for a while. I have arranged for you to be cared for by two of my disciples. I will come back for you."

What the fuck?

Where was she going? She thought she was Jesus now? She had literally lost her mind.

Still, I thought a break from her would be nice. My gut screamed that this was a bad idea. I should have run to a payphone with the quarter that I had been hoarding for an emergency for weeks right then. I hadn't always trusted my gut before. This was the very last time that I ignored it.

I don't know who they were. I don't know how deep my mother was in with them. I don't know what she got out of letting them take me for six days. Sick. Hungry. Disgusting wolves. And I certainly don't know what kind of sick fucks wanted to be inside a 13-year old girl...

I had watched movies with adults kissing. I knew that boys had penises and girls had vaginas. But, I didn't know what they were for and how they go together. I didn't have health class like normal kids. I barely knew what having a period meant.

The first time they forced themselves on me, I fought tooth and nail. I clawed and scratched and screamed. I begged to die.

There were two men. One bald, one with dark hair. I didn't recognize them from church or anywhere else. They didn't look homeless or dirty. They had ripped my clothes enough that I wouldn't be able to wear them again. The man with dark hair said that he would have to get new clothes to return me in, and scolded the other man for ruining them. The bald man said he would get new clothes from my mother. One of them made a comment about getting rope or a sedative to keep me still "next time."

Oh God... there was going to be a next time.

How long was I going to be here? What was happening? Was I bleeding? I cried so hard my eyes were swollen and bruised. It hurt so badly. I felt so dirty. I felt shameful and tarnished. Did Mom know this was happening? Was this her idea? Where was she? Where was

I? Who are these men? Why are they doing this to me? WHAT. THE. ACTUAL. FUCK. IS. HAPPENING. This was worse than being hungry or homeless. Much worse.

I was thrown in a room with a mattress on the floor when they were done with me. Something happened to me on that mattress, after my innocence had been ripped away. I broke off into a different realm of survival. I couldn't process what had just happened. I couldn't think about it. The words, "next time" rang in my head. I mentally and emotionally went to a place where I pretended I was in a different life. I put what had just happened in a box, locked it away, and pretend it never happened. It was the *only* way I could deal with the trauma in that moment.

It was the only way that I would be able to go through it again. Because I knew that it was going to happen again. I was trapped.

Babies cry. I was no baby. I had to get it together. I picked myself up off that dirty mattress and put my torn clothes back on as best I could. I banged on the door and demanded to be taken back to my mother.

The man with the dark hair opened the door and smacked me so hard I fell backwards. "Shut the fuck up!" he bellowed. I cowered, both in shock and in pain, on the mattress as he told me if I spoke to him in that tone again, he would be sure to kill me.

I thought to myself, "Not if I kill you first, you son of a bitch." I wanted to say it, but even from only one hit, I knew couldn't take another. That was the only time I had any thoughts of inflicting pain on another human being. But, these men were not human. They weren't disciples. They were monsters.

There were exactly eleven times that they raped me in that room with the dirty mattress on the floor over my six-day stay. It became a game to me. I took control of the situation by just taking it. I didn't fight. I didn't scream or cry. It became just another thing that I had to do to protect Mom and to provide for us. I put it on the list with being hungry and homeless. It was just another way I had to take care of both of us.

Despite the obvious pain and violence, I still wasn't sure what was happening. But, I knew it was wrong. I thought that if I didn't fight, I was winning in some way. The dark haired man would call me a good girl when I was obedient. It made me want to punch him in the dick. It made me want to spit on his face and call him a disgusting son of a bitch. But I didn't. That wouldn't make this present hell any better.

I was tied up in a variety of different ways with different things. I preferred the rope over the zip ties. The zip ties hurt my wrists and ankles and made it that much more painful. Sometimes it would be just one of them, sometimes it would be both.

I went to that imaginary place in my head where everything was okay, and I was a normal kid with normal parents. I wished that Mom was actually sane and we lived in a big, beautiful house and Isaiah would come over for sweet tea and sit on the porch with me. I pretended anything to get me out of that awful room with those awful men.

Often, I wondered why Mom wasn't the one on that mattress being abused and violated. Why was I the one being punished for her craziness?

I wondered where she was and when I would see her again. I wondered *if* I would ever see her again. I wondered if she did go on a mountain to prepare a fake sermon for her fake following. I wondered how she knew these men.

Every time I lay down on that dirty mattress after they were done with me, I prayed to die. I didn't want to live anymore. The first two days I prayed for salvation. But I quickly realized that no one was coming to save me. No one knew where I was. No one would ever find me. The only person who knew where I was and could protect me left me here. Feeling like I had no other choice, I prayed for death.

I was returned to my mom six days later. I was a completely different person. I was no longer a savage little adolescent girl. I was a fucking warrior. I didn't speak of what happened. She asked me how the past week had been and if I learned a lot. "Oh, definitely. I learned a whole lot," I remember replying with little affect.

She told me that she was thankful that I gave her time to go speak on the mountain with God and it was all going to pay off. She said, "I'm proud of you." I shuddered and smiled. She couldn't have known what had happened, could she? Deep down, I felt like she did. I knew that in her mind she actually believed she was doing something good for the Lord.

My God, was she wrong.

She was sick. She was allowing me to be hurt by these men. For what? For money? For some weird religious blessing? What was all of this for? I lost all hope I had in her. She was too far gone. She was no longer my protector. She no longer had my back. She was a predator. A sick, twisted predator that was wearing the human suit of someone I used to know, love, and be willing to lay down my life for. I sacrificed everything for this woman. It sure as hell wasn't to be locked up for six days with those men at her command so she could go "speak to God on a mountain."

My youth was chalking up to be savage and brutal compared to normal standards. Yet, I was awfully sheltered. I knew how to beg and sleep on the streets. I knew how to steal food, lie, and manipulate a paranoid schizophrenic, but I didn't know about sex or drugs or sick nasty men that wanted to rub their dirty penises on little girls. Why should any 13 year old know about those things?

They shouldn't.

CHAPTER 10

had never wanted to die before. I had never thought about hurting myself to feel better. I had never wished for death and fantasized about being killed, until this point. I began to seek comfort in pain. I had control over the pain I caused myself. I could control how bad it hurt, how long it lasted, how much blood it drew. It became therapy.

Along with self-harm, I wrote. A lot. I wrote about darkness and loneliness. I wrote about death and finding comfort in pain and blood. The imaginary safe and happy place in my head wasn't cutting it anymore. I used a jagged pen cap, rubber bands, and a rusty steak knife I found on the ground. I dreamed of having the courage to plunge that knife in my stomach and bleeding out for her to find me. That is what I wanted more than anything. I wanted the pain to be over and I wanted *her* to feel bad because it was all her fault.

But that desire and game plan left quickly. I realized that she would likely go to jail for the rest of her life if I wound up dead. She was so incredibly fucked up in the head that she would believe that it was God's will that I die.

I was not about to give her that satisfaction.

I wanted her to feel guilty. I wanted her to have some sense of remorse for what was happening. I wanted her to be my mom and fucking save me. But she was too far gone, and I realized that I had to save myself.

It had been three months since those men took me to that room. I was safe. We were staying with a family in Alabama from church. The mom was so kind and brought us into her home and fed us along with her three children and husband. She made the most delicious Mexican food. She would make homemade taquitos and empanadas. I must have eaten 100 of them every time she cooked for us. I was always extra thankful when there was *good* food to eat. This began my love affair with Mexican food *(I never realized that until just now, but I do love me some tacos, for real)*.

But, our welcome soon ran out because - surprise! - Mom was unbearable. I began to be unable to stand her too.

As I prepared for our next journey to find a new couch or parking lot to sleep in, something happened. This was the cherry on top of the fucked up cake Mom had been baking for the past 5 years.

She found my journal and all of my poetry.

My journal, the one I had all of my feelings written down. My poetry was all dark and destructive. It talked about death, how crazy she was, and how God isn't real. I had written about how I felt she was the devil. All of the resentment, pain, struggle and frustrated feelings that had been bottled inside of me for my entire life...they were all in that notebook.

And. She. Read. It. All.

My mother had a temper. She always had one. She had never physically laid a hand on me a day in her life. I was not physically punished growing up, until that day.

She calmly asked me to go for a walk with her down the red dirt road in Alabama one afternoon. I remember it was hot as hell. She was speaking in spiritual tongues (something she did often), so I didn't see this coming.

She pulled out my journal from underneath her shirt and threw it on the ground. Before I had a solid moment to realize what it was, she was screaming at me. The veins were bulging out of her forehead and I thought her eyes were going to pop out of their sockets. She backed me all the way down the road. "YOU ARE NO LONGER MY DAUGHTER!" she yelled. "YOU ARE NO LONGER MY DAUGHTER! YOU ARE THE DEVIL'S DAUGHTER! IF YOU WANT TO DIE, I WILL MAKE THAT HAPPEN RIGHT NOW! I WILL KILL YOU BECAUSE YOU ARE SATAN! I HATE YOU! YOU ARE THE WORST THING THAT HAS EVER HAPPENED TO ME! TODAY, YOU DIE!"

She wrapped her hands around my neck and squeezed as hard as she could. Oh, my God. She was actually trying to kill me. She *actually* wanted me dead. She meant every word she had screamed at me.

The hope of Super Mom making a return died that day. I saw no humanity left in her eyes. Her soul was gone. Her mind was officially no longer her own. My mom had been overtaken by her demons, and what stood before me was the shell of someone I used to know, trust, and look up to. I put my life on the line. I protected her. I starved for her. I was raped for her. I would probably have killed for her.

I will never forget that crazed look in her eyes that day. It was as if she were actually possessed.

In a way, this whole thing was comical because I was bigger than her. My mom was 5'2" on a good day and had incredibly frail arms from a childhood disease; she stood no chance against me. I was taller and stronger. She was physically incapable of hurting me unless I allowed her.

Don't get me wrong, the blows she made at my face with her boney knuckles hurt like hell, but my life was not in danger. That wasn't the point. She had turned on me. That day, I was done protecting her, and I was done fighting for her. I was done sacrificing everything for her. That was the day that I chose to put myself first. I was no longer her daughter and she was no longer my mother.

Despite everything I had done to keep us safe, fed, and protected, it didn't matter. It had been nearly five years and she was worse. We both were worse. I wanted to go home. I wanted to go far away from her. I wanted out.

The mother that had taken us in had said, "I am so sorry, Brittany. I love you to pieces, but I can't have your mother in this house anymore. Is there anyone I can help you contact?" This time, I said yes. I was done running. I was going the fuck home. She told me that if I wrote a letter, she would mail it. So, that is exactly what I did.

I wrote a letter to my dad telling him what had been going on and how sick mom really was. I left out a lot of it because I didn't want her to go to jail. I just wanted to get away. I just wanted to come home. I didn't want to deal with her anymore. I wanted to eat three meals a day and go to school and shower daily. I wanted to be a kid, whatever that meant. Maybe I'd finally find out.

I gave the letter to the kind woman and asked her to mail it. I told her to make sure my mom didn't find out. She mailed it. Within the next week, we were on the streets again. Mom wasn't really speaking to me since the journal/choking incident. She demanded that I rebuke the devil and repent for my sins. As if *I* was the one in the wrong. I wasn't offended or surprised. I played along to keep her from drawing any more attention to us. We didn't need that. I didn't need that.

Her humanity showed through a few times which made me panic and write a retraction letter to my dad. I said I made all of it up because Mom and I got into a fight and I was looking forward to seeing him for summer visitation soon *(This was a total crock, of course. I knew there was no way I would never make it home).*

Mom found a woman with a nice apartment who lived alone that wanted someone to clean for her. Mom worked her magical acting skills and had her agree to us moving in.

By the time we arrived, it was the longest we had gone without showers. I remember the first bath I took in the woman's beautiful white garden tub. I drew the water and sat down, enveloped in warmth. I was repulsed by how dirty I was. I had to change the water twice and eventually just ended up taking a shower. My hair was badly matted. I can assure you that I smelled horrible, but I had just become so used to my own stench.

When I turned the shower on, it was like a cloud that hit me in the face. I tried to drown out the smell with botanical shampoo. I felt like a brand new person when I got out of the bathroom. It was the most glorious feeling in the world. I will never forget it. To this day, every time I step out of the shower I'm grateful. So very grateful.

I loved this place so much. It was a beautiful community with a pool. I wished I could have stayed with this woman forever. But I knew that this was just another pit stop on the crazy train and our time here wouldn't last. I was wondering what Dad was doing since receiving the letters, but I knew we were still kept well under the radar so there was no way that anyone would find us. I felt bad about writing the letter which is why I retracted it. I knew that Mom couldn't take care of herself because she was sick and it wasn't her fault. I knew that she wouldn't make it without me. I knew that if I left, she would die.

As sure as I knew she was never going to be my Super Mom again, I knew I couldn't just leave her. I loved her more than anyone else could ever imagine. And more than anyone else ever would.

I sat by the community pool and wrote in my journal about the darkness. I sat at the end of the dock near the complex and fantasized about putting a boat rope around my neck and drowning myself.

I would listen to Avril Lavigne on my Walkman and pretend I was someone else.

Pretending was getting harder and harder to do.

I had locked away so much pain in my short 14 years that I just wasn't sure where to put it anymore. The tunnel was long and dark. The light near the end was getting further and further away. What if I had to go back to stay with those men again? What if Mom figured out a way to actually kill me?

I couldn't sleep at night worrying about those things. My heart would race and I would feel uneasy. This is when I was first began experiencing anxiety and panic attacks. I locked so many demons away that sometimes they would slip out the sides of the box and bite me. But I didn't know what else to do. I didn't have anyone I could tell, and now my journal was being closely monitored.

I began to write and put loose pieces of paper under my clothes, but I would eventually lose them and have more anxiety about Mom finding them. It was a terrible cycle.

Until I was picked up.

CHAPTER 11

t was a beautiful afternoon in March 2003. I didn't know where Mom was. I was getting ready to walk out the door, when I heard a loud knock followed by, "Police, open up!" I panicked. There was nowhere to go.

I nervously answered the door thinking that they were here for Mom. The officer asked for Brittany Cooley. "That's me," I replied. The officer was short and stocky with a black mustache. His face was as cold as stone.

The officer asked if I had any weapons on me. I had weapons, but not to hurt anyone other than myself and they weren't on me in that moment. I was confused by the question. Even though I looked like a punk because my shirt was tattered and my jeans were severely ripped-up (before that was a common fashion trend) and I wore fishnets on my arms (because Avril did), I was no delinquent. This guy had *no* clue what I had been through. I certainly had committed no crimes.

He asked if I was going to come with him willingly or if he had to handcuff me. I was shocked and scared out of my mind. What the actual fuck was this guy talking about?! He clearly had the wrong Brittany Cooley. What on earth had my mother done and where was she? I told the cop I had no problems going with him, but I didn't know what for. He said that he received papers to pick me up and there were reports that I could be found here.

Mom appeared at that moment and was in just as much shock as I was. She was a good actress, but I could tell her surprise was genuine. She didn't do this. She definitely didn't see this coming either.

I went with the officer. He placed me in the back of his squad car. The seat was hard. I was beyond terrified. Was I going to jail? Why? For what? Mom told me that she would come find me and bring me back home soon. I thought, "Yeah, right Mom. You, of all people, can't save me. Not from the police. They will see right through your bullshit."

I remember the officer grilling me about having a lighter. He asked me if I was smoking anything other than cigarettes. He asked me if I was smoking marijuana and who was dealing it to me. I didn't even know what marijuana was. I had a lighter because you have those when you grow up homeless. What the fuck!

I was so mad, but I was smart enough to know that if I acted up with him, that would only dig my grave deeper. That would only keep me away from Mom longer. She needed me. So, I politely answered all of his questions vaguely and kept my composure. If I had learned anything about living a savage life, it was that if you put up a fight, it generally made things worse.

I asked him where he was taking me. He said he was taking me downtown to The Juvenile Detention Center.

At this point, I'm a young teenager. I was homeless with a crazy mother who likely made money off of my rape, I went hungry more often than I was fed, the only clothes I had were thrift-store freebies, and the only possessions that I valued was my Walkman and my journal. The last full grade I completed was third, and I had been out of a school system for five years. I hadn't had regular medical or dental care in that length of time either.

AND *I* WAS GETTING ARRESTED?

Why wasn't Mom being taken in?! Do they know about her? Maybe I should tell them. All of these thoughts were swirling around my head as we pulled up to the facility. My first thought was, "Wow. This place looks like a prison." Because it was one... Good God, even then I knew I was about to embark on a whole new survival skill set.

Jail. That's something I haven't experienced yet.

The officer opened the car door and escorted me into the front of the building. I had no idea what was going to happen, but I knew this wouldn't be good. He handcuffed me to a seat in the waiting area in case I got the idea to run. I likely could have escaped, but even in that moment I knew how stupid that would have been.

He went to the desk and told the receptionist that he had Brittany Cooley there to be booked. I will never forget the woman at that desk. She was a big sassy black lady with crazy fingernails and a huge bun that looked like a beehive on top of her head. She wore black-framed glasses and her makeup was flawless. Her nails clacked as she typed what I assumed was my name into the system to see where I was to go.

She took off her glasses and looked at that cop like she was about to take his head off. I enjoyed every second of what happened next. She yelled, "DAMNIT ALBERT. SHE ISN'T SUPPOSED TO BE HERE. SHE IS SUPPOSED TO BE ESCORTED TO CHILDREN AND FAMILY SERVICES FOR HER CASEWORKER TO PICK HER UP! YOU TAKE THOSE DAMN CUFFS OFF HER RIGHT NOW. I AM REPORTING YOUR ASS TO YOUR SERGEANT!" She demanded that the cop give her the keys to uncuff me, and he did. His face was sorry, but he never said it. Albert was too proud to admit he fucked up big time. I knew karma would take care of him someday.

The woman came over to me and uncuffed me. So gently and sweetly she said, "I'm sorry baby, you come right over here with me to my desk. I'll get you a drink and a snack and call your caseworker to come get you here. Don't you pay that dumb cop no mind, you hear? You're safe with me."

Ah. It all made sense. My dad. The letters. Everything was falling into place. I wasn't in trouble. I was finally being saved!

Dad was going to come get me and I was going to be able to go home. I thought sending the retraction letter would have stopped him from coming to get me. I wondered if he thought I was just as crazy as Mom. I didn't know what to think. All I knew was that it was no longer in my hands. An angel had been watching over me and I was about to go home. This was all over. Finally!

Or so I had thought.

Yet again, I didn't anticipate what was going to happen next.

CHAPTER 11

My caseworker was named Shannon. She was young, maybe in her early 20's. I could tell she was fresh out of college. I liked that about her. She could sort of relate to me. I remember thinking that day that I wanted to be just like her when I grew up. I wanted to help get kids out of crazy situations like mine and put them back with their families.

She explained that her department had been looking for me or quite some time and that my family was worried sick about me. My thought was immediately, well what about Mom? Are they worried about her? I am. She won't make it without me. But I didn't want to fight to live anymore. I was so over it. I was over her. I really wanted to go home. I missed my family.

Shannon took me to lunch and then to her office. She introduced me to all of her co-workers. I asked about her job and her life. She didn't treat me like a criminal or like a dirty kid who was worthless. She talked to me like I was a human being. She talked to me like I had a sound mind. She talked to me like she had a sound mind. A real conversation with a person who wasn't crazy: I forgot how much I enjoyed that. Being stuck with mom's babble had me in a bubble like a whole different realm of cabin fever. It was fun hanging out with Shannon.

But, then she told me that I was going to live with a family while the court processed paperwork for me to go home.

Wait what? Why can't I go home with my dad? Why can't they just put me on an airplane? Or why can't he just come get me? Why do I have to stay with strangers? I don't want to stay with strangers - I want my dad!

I remember asking her these questions. She was apologetic in the answers she gave. I could tell it wasn't her decision. It was out of her hands. I wished so badly that I could go stay with her. She made me feel safe. She felt like a big sister.

The intake process was exhausting. I had to see five doctors and get all kinds of shots and tests done. I had to see a psychologist and was enrolled in intensive therapy. I had to fill out all of this paperwork and take all kinds of tests for schooling. I knew this was all going to hurt Mom. I did not disclose everything that had happened. I fluffed and sugar-coated it to show her as a struggling sick mom, not the completely demon-possessed monster that tried to kill me and let men use me like a toy and lock me in a room with the mattress on the floor.

I managed to keep the dark haired and bald man out of my intake paperwork. If I didn't talk about it, and didn't think about it, it never happened right? I never had any kind of pelvic exam done, and for that I was thankful.

I learned of these exams they do in between your legs in my first foster home from one my foster sisters, Melissa. She had to get them done because her step dad did those things to her too. It made me sick. I wanted no part of that.

One of the ladies processing my intake asked me all kinds of questions. When the question came up about anyone every touching me, I flinched inside but learned how to lie from the best liar in the world. I acted as if I didn't know anything about what that meant. On the papers, I had to answer questions like, "What do you do when you get angry or feel hurt?" My real answer was, "Cut myself and write depressing poetry about my funeral." The answer I wrote was, "I pray about it."

The truth was I wanted nothing to do with God. I never wanted to attend another church service or say a prayer again. If Mom was a servant of God and was doing his will, I wanted to renounce my belief and go to the dark side. I blamed God for her getting sick. I blamed God for the past five years. I was told that those men taking me away those six days was me being a servant to the Lord. Well, I was no longer a servant of anyone other than Brittany Cooley.

Of course, I knew I couldn't say those things so I had to say what I needed to say to appease the caseworkers and to move this process along smoothly. I assumed my stand as a prayerful young teen would make me more appealing to good families and stay under the radar. Hopefully, that would get me home faster.

This whole thing felt like bullshit. Why the fuck couldn't I just go home? I had a dad who wanted me. Mom is crazy, Dad is fine. Why is this so complicated?

I was in foster care from the day I got picked up in March 2003 until May of that same year. It was the longest two months of my life. I would be lying if i said they were the "hardest," because you already know I had been through much worse. No, it was just long and difficult. Being put into a home with people I didn't know with suddenly enforced structure, rules, and sharing space with other kids with fucked up parents was very foreign to me.

My first home was the best. I really didn't want to leave. She took me shopping for clothes and her daughter burned me CD's with all kinds of explicit rap music for my Walkman. Mom would never let me listen to any of this, which made it even better. I walked all over their beautiful neighborhood and pretended it was like being home with Dad in the middle of nowhere PA. It was so close, yet so far away.

In my time at Miss Frankie's, my first foster mother, I learned a lot from my foster sisters. They were both younger than me and had a rough go at it. They were biological sisters. The one little girl wasn't more than 7 years old. I felt bad for them and their story. After learning what their step dad did to them, I was thankful that I didn't know the men who did that to me.

All three of us girls slept in the same room. There were three beds. It was like a sleepover every night. Sometimes we would push the beds together so we could all be closer. It was a sense of comfort for us all. We had all been through hell.

One night, Melissa asked me if I was still awake. Of course I was. I couldn't sleep. I was an insomniac with severe anxiety. My mind never shut off. She asked me if she could tell me a secret. I said, of course. She told me that she thought girls were pretty. I thought, well girls are pretty. She went a step further and told me that she wanted to kiss girls on the lips. I didn't know what to say. My face flushed. I felt something...foreign. Something exotic. I couldn't explain it.

I saw two girls kissing before and thought it was strange. I was taught that you were supposed to only kiss boys and only after you were married. Then I thought, well I kind of want to kiss a girl sometimes too, but I didn't say that. I would never admit that to her. I just said, "Oh... I see. Well, we had better get to sleep." And that was the end of that.

The next day Melissa's little sister educated me on "blow dries." Apparently that was when you put a boy's "thing" in your mouth and suck on it like a lollipop. I was absolutely disgusted at the thought. I couldn't imagine doing that. It was bad enough that the bald man and dark haired man touched me with it. I would have bit it off if they made me do that. Pee comes out of there! That's disgusting!

I was nauseated for the next few days. She wasn't even seven and she was forced to experience and know what "blow dries" were. Looking back, it makes my heart breaks for that little girl, and I often wonder whatever happened to her.

I had to go to school for the last few weeks of the school year due to Florida State Law. I was now in custody of the state. A state had custody of me. It was a scary thought to say the least.

I didn't know what to do in school. The last full grade I completed was third and being thrown right into eighth grade at the end of the year was a mistake. Whoever made that call, it was a bad one.

I was bullied and made fun of. Not that I cared because you have far thicker skin than the average teenager when you grow up having a childhood like mine. But that still doesn't mean it was pleasant.

I honestly didn't even try to fit in. There were a few girls who tried to be my friends, but I stuck with my foster sister, Melissa, instead of branching out. She was the only thing close to a friend that I had. I just wanted to go home. I didn't want to make friends, or plant roots, or do well in school. I just wanted to not be in Florida anymore. I wanted to go home and be with my dad.

When Miss Frankie went on sabbatical shortly after we arrived, my placement was moved to the next foster home. I didn't have such good luck at this house. The woman at my second foster home was mean. Nasty. Downright evil.

I got in trouble for everything. I didn't clean the toothpaste out of the sink one morning - because having a toothbrush and brushing my teeth daily was new to me - so I didn't really clean up well. She locked me in my room for nearly ten hours and only allowed me to come out only to eat. I remember walking on eggshells and feeling as though I had to keep to myself and stay out of the way.

I swam in the pool while she was at work. I made sure to eat before she got home and clean up well after myself. I stayed in my room most of the time. I didn't come out unless asked. I knew if I screwed up my placement, I would screw up my chances of getting home. I had to get home. There was finally a light at the end of the tunnel. I wasn't about to let this bitch screw it up.

Mom had supervised visitation with me weekly. It was awkward because I had to sit in a room that was being video recorded with a caseworker. Mom would try to whisper weird shit to me and she would get scolded. She would openly talk shit about the system and the caseworkers in front of them, loudly. I thought to myself that if she wanted to get me back, she wasn't doing a very good job.

She hated the clothes that I wore and said I looked like a Jezebel. This was the holy way to call me a slut. I thought she was jealous that I have new clothes. I felt bad for thinking that, but I knew it was the truth. She took everything away from me and she could no longer do that.

My grandparents came down and took care of Mom while I was in foster care. I remember them coming to visitation and seeing me with Mom. I loved them fiercely, and was so happy that they were there for her because I couldn't be. I felt guilty but it was a relief to finally have a promised bed and three meals a day. Soon I would be going home, to Dad.

Shannon prepared me for court. I had to go to court and testify in front of a judge in order to go home under my Dad's care. Shannon said that it was important that I didn't lie, and it was important that I said what I really wanted, no matter what.

I was nervous about court. I knew there had been court hearings in the past that had to do with me, but I was never at them. I didn't know what to expect, but I knew that was the last obstacle I had to hurdle to get home.

They brought me into the courtroom, and there she sat. I was horrified. I didn't know she was going to be there. I didn't know I had to tell the judge and everyone what had happened in front of her. That was something I wasn't willing to do. It would crush her. It would break her. If she thought I was the devil's child before when she read my journal, she would feel more betrayed now.

As much as I wanted to leave and knew she was in the wrong, I didn't want to make it that real. My heart jumped into my throat and I panicked. I wanted to run out, but I knew there was nowhere for me to go. I knew I couldn't stay with that mean foster lady anymore, and there was *no* chance of me going back with Mom. She told me in our visitation that Grandpa and Grandma were there to help her get a place to live so I could stay with her. I, of course, thought this was a complete lie. There was no way on earth that they would want me to stay with such a monster, even when the monster was their own daughter.

I had to do this. I had to put the final nail in the coffin that would set me free. I gave myself a pep talk and took the stand.

"Brittany, can you please place your right hand on the bible and answer the following question? Do you swear to tell the truth, the whole truth, and nothing but the truth so help you God?"

So, help me God.

Yes. Got it. The problem with that question was that I didn't believe in a God that would make my mom so crazy. My promise was invalid.

Instead of making my mom look bad, I made myself look bad. I took as much of the blame as I could because she was sitting right in front of me. Staring at me. It was the same look she gave me five years ago in that hotel room in South Carolina when she lied to grandma for the first time.

I told the courtroom that I exaggerated in the letter. I said I was angry when I wrote it. It was after we had gotten into a disagreement. I remember saying "Typical mother daughter stuff." That was a joke. I don't even know what "typical mother daughter stuff" was. Was it, like, going and getting nails done and having a movie date? Is that what we were supposed to do? I had no idea.

But, like my mother, I was a good liar. When the attorney asked me if she had physically harmed me, "choked me" like I had written in the letter, I said no. I said that was a lie and she never hurt me. When I was asked if I wanted to go home to live with my father, I said yes. I looked at Mom and watched her heart break. But I had done that to Dad enough over the years and I owed it to him. I owed it to myself. The truth was, I wanted nothing more than to leave this monster behind and start a new life with my dad.

The truth also was I had a wealth of experiences to share that would put my mom in jail for a long, long time. It wouldn't matter if she claimed mental illness; she would undoubtedly be put away for the truth. Instead, I chose to show her mercy. I didn't want to hurt her the way she hurt me. I just wanted to get out and far away.

I hugged her after court and she cried. I felt nothing. I was numb. Eventually, I felt relief that it was over and I was going to go home. I shuddered at the thought of what she had told me about my grandparents giving her a place to live so I could stay with her. God, I hoped that wasn't true. I wouldn't survive another round of hell with her. I didn't have it in me. I threw in the towel. I was done. I gave her all I had. I had nothing left. It was finally *my* turn.

Not even a week later I was being escorted on an airplane. HOME. I had a flight attendant that stayed with me the whole time because I was too young to fly alone. I had to wear a button and I got extra snacks and drinks. When the plane took off, it was healing for me. It was officially happening. I could leave the craziness behind. To this day, one of my favorite feelings in the whole world is taking off into the air. That feeling of letting shit go... it's powerful. Even now, I still feel a beautiful freedom when I travel, particularly on airplanes.

I was relieved, but the closer I got to my destination, my anxiety crept in and became nearly suffocating. I began to worry about what would happen to Mom. I was worried about Dad and his new girlfriend liking having me around. I was worried about having to go back to school and start the fourth grade as a 14-year old. I was worried that something would happen and I would wake up back in the room with the mattress on the floor, blindfolded, and being taken back to Mom's parked car. I was worried that God would punish me for leaving her all alone when I lost my feelings of obligation to protect her.

I closed my eyes, put on my headphones, and drowned out the shuddering thoughts with my vulgar rap music.

The plane landed in the afternoon at Wilkes Barre/Scranton International Airport. The attendant walked me off the plane and escorted me to baggage claim where my father awaited me. All of my anxiety subsided the minute I saw his face.

I'll never forget the look on his face. It was a mixture of pure happiness and relief. His eyes were kind and tired. I could tell that he had been through hell too. This whole process wasn't easy for him either. The years of worry, all of the times I broke his heart and chose Mom over him, over and over again, were exhausting for him. He had felt like he played second string to my Mom since that day we were set to go camping all those years ago and I changed my mind.

Sadly, a lot of kids in the foster care system didn't have someone to save them. I was lucky I did. My hero. My Dad.

I finally chose him.

I chose me.

I chose life.

And I was grateful that I had family to go to.

I ran into his arms and squeezed him as tight as I could. "Let's go home!"

I'll never forget how well I slept that night in my own bed. In my own room. In my house tucked away in the woods of Northeastern Pennsylvania.

CHAPTER 12

Dad said two things to me when I first arrived home: 1. I will be going to school at Wyalusing Valley Junior/Senior High School in the fall. 2. He was going to marry his girlfriend, Sylvia.

I was more concerned about the first thing but the second ended up being more of a challenge. *This book isn't about my evil step mother - though that's exactly what she became. I will leave it at that.*

School. Oh, how I dreaded school. Outside of the small fraction of formal schooling I had in the last five years, the last official grade I had attended was third. I was now 14-years old and supposed to be going into ninth grade.

My concern wasn't the academics. It was the structure. I didn't know how to be told what to do. I didn't know how to act around "normal kids." Who knew what they had heard about me and I knew some of them would remember me from grade school.

To say I was nervous didn't even begin to cover it.

There was a lot to get through before I could walk through the doors. My aunt is the other hero of this book. Along with my dad, she fought tooth and nail for my best interest and did everything in her power to see that I got where I needed to go and had everything I needed to succeed, despite my circumstances. I can honestly say that I would not be where I am today and I would have never graduated or gone on to college without her in my corner.

My aunt was a pusher. There was no mercy. There was no favoritism or coddling. I was expected to rise up and meet what lay ahead of me. She pulled every single string she had to get the school district to give me a chance. A kid with a history of trauma and no transcripts since third grade didn't really have a fair shot at any kind of stream-lined education.

I took standardized tests for days, and I'm sure that I did awful on all of them. Tests were the worst - especially on shit I had never learned. I barely knew my multiplication tables and there were math problems with symbols that I had never seen before. Clearly the only solution was to color in bubbles so they made a pattern. That was the only thing I could do.

My aunt made the school board a promise that I would study over the summer and begged them to give me a chance. She also found me a math tutor in her neighborhood and made sure I was prepared to cram as much knowledge into my brain over the summer as possible so I would be ready for school in the fall. I thought she was crazy. Not crazy like Mom, but crazy for believing in me. She actually thought I could pull it off and start ninth grade in only a few months' time.

She never showed me any pity. She treated me like I was one of her own children. She was the proud mother of two incredibly beautiful and intelligent girls. Both were honor students and athletes. They excelled in every area of life that they possibly could and more. Every time she spoke of them, she would glow like they were shiny trophies that she could share and show off to the world.

I felt like a black sheep next to my cousins. They were not only smart and strong and talented, they were also kind. They both had very different personalities, but each lit up any room that they were in. I wanted to grow up and be just like them. I believed I had a shot at being on their level because of the way Aunt Val treated me. I wanted her to glow when she talked about me too. "My niece, Brittany Danielle...what a strong, smart, talented girl." I dreamed of hearing her say that. That summer, it was motivation to work hard and catch up academically on all I'd missed.

I didn't want special treatment. Not really. I didn't want to spill my guts to her or anyone about what had gone on in Florida. I didn't want anyone to feel sorry for me. I knew my family had already gone through enough worrying about me for nearly half a decade. After all was said and done, I was fine. I made it home. I survived. It was my cross to bear. If anyone felt badly, it should be my mother. What the rest of my family didn't know wouldn't hurt them.

I had no idea that my silence would come back and hurt me. We aren't to that chapter yet. There are still a few years before it catches up with me.

Despite not getting a formal education for much of my time in Florida, I never felt stupid. I knew I was smart, just in different ways. I realized that most 14-year olds had not had the life experiences that I did. My "homework" was trying to find food without stealing it from stores, avoiding child protective services, and making sure I never ran out of batteries for my Walkman. Math was in no way relevant to my life on the streets. I knew how to survive, not how to be a normal kid. This traditional learning stuff seemed like rocket science. But I wanted to be someone that made my family proud. I didn't want to turn out like my mom. I didn't want to be pitied and I didn't want anyone to make excuses for me. I wanted to rise up and shine.

Mr. Murphy tutored me in my aunt's kitchen every week. He was a retired math teacher that lived next door. I hated every minute of it, but I did it and put my best foot forward. I did it for my aunt because if she believed in me so much, then I must be capable. She was successful and so were her daughters. If I was going to fit in around here, I had to pull my weight.

I heard from Mom through phone calls and lots of letters. She would say that she couldn't wait until I could come back home. I kept saying, "Me too, Mom" only because I knew she really believed that I would come back to her.

I truly believed that she did miss me. I really believed that she didn't mean to cause me so much pain. I wanted to believe that she didn't know what those men did to me when she lent me to them for nearly a week of hell. Maybe she really thought they took me to pray and I was serving the Lord. That doesn't change the reality that she did hurt me countless times and in countless ways. On purpose or not, I knew with my whole being that Super Mom was dead and gone for good with no hope of making a return or comeback. She was gone.

My mom wasn't well and wasn't willing to get help. Her letters made less and less sense with each that was delivered. I was trying to move on and I just couldn't. She wouldn't let me. Her letters were reminders of everything I had experienced and I wanted to lock it in a box and throw away the key. I wanted to drown the box in the bottom of the ocean and start over. I wished that she would leave me alone. I wished that she would let me drown the box. But every time she called or wrote, she made it all real again. It didn't matter how much music I listened to or how many walks I took. She was there, haunting me.

As the days went by, I began to adjust to a new life that wasn't harmful or destructive. I was around many adults that held a sound mind. They weren't paranoid or crazy. I didn't have to beg for food or dig in garbage cans. There was a refrigerator full at all times. There was no one lurking in the shadows to avoid. I was behind a locked door each night with electricity and the ability to shower daily. It was a whole new way of living.

The day finally came when my aunt got clearance for me to be admitted into the ninth grade. I had a chance to prove myself to her and the school district that I could maintain a ninth-grade level curriculum. I was to be put in every ninth grade subject aside from math. I would be placed in a seventh grade remedial math class due to my incredibly low test scores. I was so happy with those results. I could deal with being behind in one class. I was given a chance!

I still didn't care what others thought of me. I never had to before. I had missed out on social status and school politics. Maybe that develops somewhere in middle school. But for me, I had no idea what I was walking into. I just knew that I was thankful to be walking somewhere that wasn't Mom's car to sleep.

I decided that I wanted to play volleyball. I had a friend who lived up the road that was playing and encouraged me to join too. Volleyball seemed like a great contribution to my fresh start. I had not been able to stick with softball during my time in Florida, so it had been five years since I was a part of any kind of organized sport or extra-curricular activity. I was determined to rise above the past five years and do something fun.

How hard could it be?

A few weeks before high school officially started, practices began early at 8:00 am. I was excited to go the first day. But when I got there, I realized I was way out of my league - not to mention way out of shape! I hadn't done any kind of physical exercise other than walk since I was on the track and field team in elementary school.

The gymnasium was huge. There were over a dozen girls there. I was thankful for my friend because without her, I wouldn't have made it through that morning. That was the *only* volleyball practice I made it to. We didn't play volleyball - we ran. We ran and ran and ran some more. Shuttle sprints, suicide sprints, death sprints, and some more sprints.

I remember wanting to quit by my second lap around the gym in the warm up. It was awful. I couldn't understand why these girls were willingly doing this. They were going to actually come back and do this all over again?! I was the slowest and nearly threw up. I was so slow that the coach made everyone run again as punishment.

The coach scared the living bejesus out of me, too. He was so serious. I thought we were going to learn how to play volleyball. I don't recall there even being a volleyball on the court that day.

The next day I woke up in so much pain, I couldn't even dream of going back for more. I thought to myself, I bet no one goes back to that torture chamber of specialized hell. My legs were so sore I had to slide down the stairs on my butt. I had never felt such physical agony in my life.

If you missed one practice you were off the team. I knew that. I still didn't go. You couldn't pay me to go back there.

After 24 hours of limping around, I felt like a failure and a disappointment. I thought maybe I could go back and try again. I thought maybe there would be volleyballs. I thought maybe Coach Holdrege would make an exception. I remember him saying at the end of the practice the first day that we should all be happy to be there because, "volleyball girls were always the hottest." He didn't mean it in a dirty, pervy way but in a confident, badass way. I wanted to be a hot, badass volleyball girl.

I sheepishly walked back in the gym on the third day of practice. I saw the look in Coach's eyes and knew I had no chance in hell. He didn't even have to say anything. His facial expression said it all. I handed him my kneepads and walked my sorry ass out of the gym and never ran another lap for that man again.

I certainly felt like a disappointment, but I was also relieved because I wouldn't have to do any of that running bullshit ever again. At the end of the day, no one told me what to do. No one made me do anything that I didn't want to.

I blamed it on Mom. I was pale, had bad eyebrows, frizzy hair, and was out of shape because of her. It made me feel better to blame her for a little while. But eventually, using her as a scapegoat would get old. For now? It was easy.

It was the first day in a real high school for both me and my friend that lived up the road. She had gone to a private Christian school for her elementary and middle school education like I did for that brief period that I returned to Pennsylvania. I kind of felt like she and I were in the same boat, being new kids, but she had a little bit of an edge because she had already made friends from the volleyball team.

Boys gave her a lot of attention because she was pretty. I felt ugly next to her, but I accepted it. I blamed that on Mom too. I was ugly, out of shape, weird, and not as smart as I should be. It was all *her* fault. Not mine.

CHAPTER 13

The first day of school I was overwhelmed. There were nine periods in the school day and I had to go to a different room for each. I had a locker assigned to put my books and backpack in. Luckily, no one was mean to me. I reconnected with some friends that I had way back in elementary school. It was so strange to see the same people as teenagers. I felt like I was in the twilight zone. Maybe I blacked out and all of that crazy shit in Florida never happened.

I could only wish.

Everyone settled into their cliques. I had a hard time fitting into any of them. I wasn't pretty enough to be with the popular girls, I wasn't smart enough to be with the geeks, and I sure wasn't an athlete to fit in with the jocks. I was a weirdo. A black sheep. I could kick anyone's ass with my hands tied behind my back, but knew better than to display violence.

My skill set included manipulating paranoid schizophrenics, dodging cops and caseworkers, pretending I was someone or somewhere else to deal with trauma, sleeping on the street comfortably, finding food in garbage cans, and stealing food without getting caught. I had read the bible cover-to-cover twice along with hundreds of other books and was fluent in any and all cuss words. Still, I was struggling with wanting to be well liked and making friends.

How was I going to pull this off? The abruptness of the transition was like none of it had ever happened. From third grade, to hell, and back to ninth.

Well, it didn't matter what it felt like. I had to do this. Aunt Val said so. I disliked taking orders from anyone in my life at that point, but her orders were always non-negotiable. I knew that I had walked a hard path and there wasn't one single person in that school that would ever survive a day in my shoes. I held that close to me when things got hard and I wanted to cry. When I would catch myself feeling sorry for myself, I put on my headphones and pretended that I was a normal kid...whatever that meant.

I went through a goth phase as my freshman year progressed. My music taste went from explicit gangster rap and pop to explicit heavy metal. My headphones looped bands like KoRn, Nickelback, Evanescence, Breaking Benjamin, Three Days Grace, Seether, and any other band that sang/screamed about death, sadness, and destruction. The more screwed up the song was, the better it made me feel. I even started to write again. Dark, deep, fucked up poetry.

I made friends with the other black sheep who dressed in dark clothing and listened to similar music. I steered clear of the volleyball
girls and everyone else I couldn't relate to. I even got a boyfriend.
Actually, I had a few. I didn't know what having a boyfriend meant;
I just knew that I needed one because everyone else had one too.
Holding hands down the hallway and having notes written for me
kind of made me feel special. It never lasted though and I got bored
quickly. Nothing physical ever happened with those boys.

I continued to self-harm. I began smoking cigarettes because that's
what my friends were doing. It made me feel cool *(It wasn't cool. It
was a nasty habit that it took me nearly 11 years to kick)*. I had my first
beer. I smoked my first bowl. I was a total rebel, breaking all the rules
because that's all I ever knew how to do well. I colored outside of the
lines my whole life. Structure, listening to adults, and taking orders
was some kind of new hell for me.

I know, it sounds like I was on a downward slope of self-destruction. But remember, it was the only way I knew how to cope. When I
smoked weed and drank beer, I felt numb. I liked the way that felt. It
masked the pain I was experiencing inside. I would look at all of the
popular kids and just feel so far away from them. They weren't mean.
I was never bullied (to my face at least), but I just felt like I didn't
belong. In reality, I was making myself not belong almost on purpose
to confirm that I was the furthest thing from normal there was.

Looking back, I can only imagine what the conversations about me
among my family were like behind closed doors. My aunt told me
recently that she had asked her daughters if this was a "phase" I was
going through and wondered if it would pass. They assured her that
it would. Honestly, they didn't even know the half of it.

My cousin was right about me being in a passing phase. I look back and am thankful that no one in my family judged me. No one made me feel weird for the way that I dressed or the music that I listened to. My dad always wore black, but he was referred to as Johnny Cash. In a way, I felt like I was emulating him. Although, I never saw him wear fishnets on his arms…

Somehow, I passed ninth grade and made it through my first quarter of high school. BARELY. I certainly didn't make honor roll or get any A's, but I passed on to tenth grade which was all I really hoped for. It was a miracle. I did it.

Sophomore year came and something in me changed. I realized if I could live on the streets and take care of my mom and do all of those incredibly difficult things that no one I knew could do, then I could do something as simple as "fit in." It was almost a challenge that I had accepted. Not that I cared too much about being popular, but I wanted to be well liked by everyone. I had previously earned the nickname Queen of the Damned. I wanted to change that, I just didn't know how yet.

Aunt Val took me shopping for a new outfit and out to eat every month or so. I had previously shopped in the black section of any store with most of my wardrobe from stores like PacSun or Hot Topic.

One Saturday, I took a detour from my usual and went into Aeropostale. I walked over to a button down pinstripe shirt that was pink, white, and pastel green. I had never bought or owned anything pink, nor had I wanted to. Pink was a *happy* color. Vibrant. Girly. Feminine. A color that popular girls wore. Aeropostale was a store I felt as though I didn't belong in, until that day. I showed Aunt Val the shirt and told her I liked it. I think she was just as shocked as I was.

That day in the Johnson City Mall was a game-changing realization for me. I could be whoever I wanted. I didn't have to be Queen of the Damned. I could truly put my darkness away and just be normal. It was like a costume. I didn't really know who I was, but I knew who I wanted to be. In that moment, I hung those dark demons up in the closet and chose a different outfit. I embraced who I wanted to be by making that choice and simply made a decision to be her.

I discovered that being busy was the only way I could function. I dove in and became a part of nearly everything I could. I discovered the busier and more social I was, the less I thought about my past. I still got letters and calls from Mom, but it was a distant memory, maybe even a nightmare.

I drowned out the memories by making new ones and actually having a normal life. It's all I ever wanted - to just be a normal kid and feel fundamentally unaffected by all the shit that had happened to me. Most importantly, I never wanted anyone to know just how damaged I was. Because despite my poker face, I was still incredibly damaged underneath it all.

I became a social butterfly and was friends with mostly everyone. I realized if I was nice to people, people would be nice back. *What a novel concept.* I was called a brown-noser a few times, but I didn't care because I wanted to be liked by everyone so badly that it didn't matter. When someone felt valued or thankful for something I did for them, it made me feel good. I became addicted to that feeling. That people-pleasing feeling.

I gave it my all to pretend to sympathize with my friends when they were upset. Teenagers are the most dramatic beings on earth. Almost everything that didn't go their way was the end of the world. I found it incredibly difficult to sympathize with their petty bullshit.

They had no idea what it was like to truly struggle. They had no idea what the end of the world was really like. I did. I knew that. I lived that. The things that I would hear my classmates complain about made me roll my eyes so far back into my head, I saw my brain. It angered me that many of them were so ungrateful. I had deep seeded bitterness towards those who complained about clothes, shoes, or not having a bigger allowance.

Despite flourishing against the odds, a huge part of me felt like I was drowning. I was so tired from trying to be friends with everyone and make everyone proud of me. I never felt as though I would be caught up from all of the years that I had missed. I never felt like I was on anyone else's level. I always felt as though I had to prove something to someone.

I tried to bury the past and pretend like I was normal, but inside I knew that was complete bullshit. My past was locked away but it subconsciously haunted me. I wanted to distance myself so far away from what had happened to me and create a new life where no one knew any of it.

I did a good job. I don't think anyone other than my family knew what I had been through while I was on my five-year long "vacation" in Florida. Even family didn't know the extent of what happened. I had planned to never tell them either. They didn't need to know. No one needed to bear the burden or feel sorry for me. I was fine. I was more than fine. I was in high school and thriving.

Most importantly, I was not my mother.

The only time I ever felt like I wasn't a black sheep with all kinds of problems was when I was under the influence. So, being under the influence became my new favorite pastime. Party Brittany lived for over a decade before she was put to rest. She's had a few flare ups here and there after that too.

I drank and smoked to feel normal. It's the only thing that I had that offered any kind of relief to the imposter syndrome that I felt. In high school, it was also fun. It activated the bad girl in me. I was way underage and knew if I got caught I would get my ass kicked. The more I drank, the more badass I felt.

Every time I got away with it, I wanted to do it more. I felt as though I was entitled to do these things and break rules. I had gone through hell... I earned the right to feel good! Of course, I knew that no one in my family would see it that way.

In the middle of my junior year, my life experienced a massive plot twist. My mom decided to return home to Pennsylvania.

CHAPTER 14

She had agreed to come home after much begging and pleading from my grandparents. They were distraught. We knew she was destitute. We knew she wouldn't make it. I also begged her to come home and get help. I did because I was her daughter and I was worried about her. Yet at the same time, a huge part of me never wanted to see her again. After what I had endured with her and after how hard I worked at rebuilding my life to be normal, I didn't want her to ruin all the progress that I had made.

The last few months we spent together were something out of a horror film. I had been trying to forget all of it. I knew she couldn't hurt me. I knew things would never go back to the way they were, but she was a physical, human reminder of what I had endured and what I had lost.

She was sicker than ever, mentally and physically. Nothing she said on the phone or in her letters made sense and she lived in a completely different dimension than the rest of the world. I was so nervous to see her again after so much time had passed, but I truly did want her to be okay.

But I knew she wasn't. That's what scared me.

I didn't know what would be waiting in my grandmother's dining room when I arrived that night to see her for the first time since that day in court. I had talked with her and received dozens of letters, but she was a memory that I tried to distance myself from. It was the only way I knew how to cope with my past.

I remember driving my 1996 Chevy Corsica down my grandparents' driveway the evening that she had arrived. My heart was pounding out of my chest.

I vividly remember looking at her for the first time in three years. I didn't recognize her. She was incredibly frail. She couldn't have weighed any more than 82 pounds. Her skin was tanned like leather. Her eyes bulged from her head. Her hair was short and poofy. It looked as if she cut it herself with a rusty razor blade.

Her voice cracked when she spoke, "Hi, Baby Bird." I nearly fainted. It was her. It really was. She looked nothing like the mom I had when I was a little girl. She looked nothing like the woman that I had left. She was a skeleton covered in tanned skin that sounded just like her. It nearly broke me.

I left her to better myself. I left her to have a life and go to school and get out of the hell I had faced. I left her to ensure that I would never face those hardships or go without ever again. I left her because she hurt me. I left her because she let those men take me. I left her because I wouldn't have survived another one of her visits to Mount Zion.

Even though I had constantly worried about leaving her because I knew she couldn't take care of herself, I never allowed myself to think about what would happen to her once I left her. I realized that what I had said to my father that broke his heart over and over again was true. "I can't leave Mom. She will die without me. She won't make it. She needs me."

I had thought about suicide many times before prior to this night, but I began to seriously consider that being the only release for the pain I felt when I heard her soft, faint, sweet but broken voice.

I had only been gone three years and this is what happened to her. While I was dancing on football fields, being a glutton with food, and acting like a teenage asshole with my friends, she was slowly dying. I sometimes catch myself wondering what happened to her in those three years after I left, but I truly don't want to know. Her version of reality of what took place and what actually happened were polar opposite things. The only way I could know was if I were there. I felt so guilty. The guilt ate me alive. I was absolutely sick. It was so painful to look at her and hear her speak and watch her move. Selfishly, I couldn't bear it.

I regret to tell you that I spent as little time with her as I possibly could while she was in Pennsylvania. It is one of the deepest regrets that I have to this day. I worked hard to become a "normal kid" with a "normal life." Every time I saw her, she reminded me that I wasn't a normal kid and made me feel as though I could never have a normal life. I felt damaged and broken and all of the horrible memories that I locked away in my box of darkness flooded out every time I looked at her. I had mastered the art of pretending my problems and past didn't exist, but seeing her ruined that and I felt like I had to start again from ground zero.

During the time Mom was home, my grandfather was diagnosed with lung cancer. She cared for him and kept my grandmother company. Grandma and Grandpa enjoyed having her home so much. The happiness in my grandmother's face was worth the difficulty of seeing Mom. She was making her so happy. My grandmother spent her life caring for, worrying about, and going to the ends of the earth and extremes to ensure her daughter's safety and wellbeing. I was happy that she finally seemed happy again.

I admire her strength and the love she had for my mother. It was so inspiring to me. They say the love of a mother is like no other. My grandmother was 100% living proof of that. The five years we were away broke my grandparents' hearts. Having Mom home with them healed that partially, I think. Mom being with Grandma during Grandpa's illness was a gift.

My grandfather passed away in 2006. Our family was broken again. He was the only grandfather I had the privilege of knowing. My paternal grandfather passed away when my dad was only sixteen. I am so thankful that Mom was with Grandma during this time.

My grandfather's funeral was the first I had ever attended. I refused to go up to the casket and say goodbye. There wasn't much I was afraid of at this point in my life, but being close to a lifeless body of such an important man that did so much for me was at the top of that list.

I cried so much that my eyes were swollen shut for days afterward. Everyone kept saying they were so sorry for our loss. I knew they meant it, but it didn't make it hurt any less. I had never lost someone to death before. This was a whole new feeling of darkness. Along with all of the hard emotions that I had felt in my life that were too overwhelming, I shoved them into a box and pushed them away. It's the only way I knew how to cope with anything. Just. Forget. About. It. Or, at least try. I didn't realize how destructive this was at the time, but I paid for it dearly later.

I went about the rest of my life as best I could. I still danced and ran track and I even made the senior basketball cheerleading squad, my greatest high school accomplishment. My cheer coaches are still two of my favorite people on earth. Head Coach will never know what she did for my life, granting me a place on that squad. It was more than just a uniform, pom-poms and a stereotype. It was proof that I could be whatever I wanted to be despite those awful years in my past despite being Gothica, Queen of the Damned just three years before. It also connected me to the most amazing girls. I felt like I was a part of something and I felt like I belonged.

Mom hit a downward spiral the week right before my senior trip to Virginia Beach. She had been stashing food under her bed and isolating. She wasn't showering. Self-destruction was setting in. I remember begging her to get help and she refused. Grandma and I were beside ourselves. We called the ambulance to take her in because her physical health was in danger. I remember the night before my senior trip, nearly missing my bus to instead be carrying her frail body down my grandma's steps and placing her on a stretcher to go to the Robert Packer Hospital to be examined.

My cousin and I followed and spoke with the psychiatrist. Nearly five hours later, and with about eight pages of handwritten proof that she had been self-destructing, we got her 302ed (involuntarily committed) to the behavioral science unit.

I felt guilty for attending my senior trip, but I was thankful she was in a facility and safe. She was no longer a danger to herself if she was there. I remember my dad telling me that I had better go on that trip and enjoy myself. That Mom wasn't my responsibility. Even after all this time, I couldn't help but think that she was. She always had been. She was the reason I existed.

I remember her being in that facility for weeks. She made no progress because she refused medication and refused to attend sessions. She was angry for us putting her there.

I visited her several times. She had upset me so badly one time; I couldn't get out of the unit fast enough. She mentioned her visit to Mount Zion and that she had sacrificed everything to make sure I could be a spoiled brat. Her words boiled my blood so hot I nearly puked right there at her bedside. I got up and sped out as fast as I could. Everything was behind lock and key and you needed a guard to get you down the elevator and out. I remember telling the nurses at the desk that I needed to leave, as Mom trailed and yelled behind me. One of them sympathetically looked at me saying, "Bad visit, hun?" She had no idea.

Eventually Mom was released on good behavior and she made an agreement with Grandma that she would take her medication and abide by her rules. I distanced myself even further from her then. She reminded me that she wasn't my mom anymore, once again, and that it was a monster that infected her mind and stood in her place.

I don't remember Mom attending many of my school events. It was better that way. I understood and was okay with it. Dad was always my biggest fan and came to everything he could, even the track meets where I frolicked around with my friends and never placed. He still came, and he was still proud. I did feel bad that he wouldn't brag about how good his daughter was at sports or school, but he never made me feel like a disappointment. Not once.

Overall I had an amazing high school career. I may be biased but, I thought I did pretty awesome for a kid who went through hell. No one could even tell. I didn't graduate at the top of my class or with honors. I didn't graduate with a letterman's jacket, but I graduated on time in June of 2007 with a long list of friends and accomplishments and experiences that I was incredibly proud of. I wished there was a survivor award, or Most Likely To Fail But Still Succeed award. I totally would have won that.

Walking across that gym stage and being handed my diploma was a feeling I'll never forget. Every time I hear the graduation song, I tear up like a little bitch because I remember how I felt that day. Seeing my dad and my Aunt in the crowd and the look on their faces was priceless and worth it all.

Aunt Val made college a non-negotiable. I did want to go, but with my SAT and ACT scores.... it didn't seem possible. But, if there is anyone more stubborn and determined than me to find a way to make something happen, it's Aunt Val. Where there is a will, Aunt Val finds a way.

I didn't have a college fund or a savings account. I had the worst scores on both standardized tests, despite taking them twice. Academics and test-taking weren't demons that I conquered, nor wanted to conquer if I am being completely honest. My life to this point had been geared around survival and just making it through. I tried my hardest to give those tests my all, but they defeated me.

Where doors close, windows open. My Aunt is the best window-finder in the entire world. Especially for her kids.

I applied for several schools, all of which I was denied. After doing research, my Aunt found a program that might be a good fit. Lock Haven University of Pennsylvania had a summer program called E.O.P. (Educational Opportunities Program). It allowed certain students to come in and take three summer courses to be admitted into the fall semester upon passing.

I applied for the program and met with the Office of Admission. I loved the campus and the people. It felt, right. It was in a small town in central Pennsylvania that was only two hours from home. It was a small state school, beautifully built on the West Branch of the Susquehanna River and Bald Eagle Creek. I saw myself going there.

CHAPTER 15

Receiving the acceptance letter into Lock Haven University's E.O.P. was another incredibly proud moment of mine. I didn't see it as a program for the academically challenged. I saw it as an opportunity for me to prove myself, once again. Bad SAT scores? No problem.

I was moved into Russell Hall and began classes soon after high school graduation. I had friends from high school that had gotten regular acceptance and were coming in the fall, so I had to prove myself so I could come back with them. I instantly hit it off with my roommate and we became the best of friends. During E.O.P. I met some amazing people, had too much fun, and passed the courses to receive my fall acceptance. I also rekindled my love for rap music and was taught how to "Walk It Out" and "Pop Lock and Drop It." I was beyond excited to be given a chance to be a real college student. Once again, Brittany Cooley defies the odds and prevails.

I originally wanted to study law and become a lawyer just like my Uncle Rich. I have failed to mention him thus far, but he is another incredibly important influencer that shaped my future. I worked for him for five summers as an Office Assistant. I learned so much and grew a whole new respect for what he did for a living. He was a real life superhero to me. I wanted to make him proud and follow in his footsteps.

Then I discovered a passion that was truly my purpose where I could make the most difference: Social Work. I could become a caseworker and save kids from abuse and neglect and give them stable homes and make sure that no one was ever left behind. I could become the person I needed. I could help make the system a better place for kids who struggled in any area of life. I knew about that life, I lived that life, I could relate on more than one level.

I was excited to use my struggles and past for good. I knew in my heart of hearts that I was meant to help kids, just like me. I was proud that I had come that far, and knew that if I could do it, anyone would. I even thought, maybe I could write a book someday sharing my childhood story to be implemented in the curriculum across the country as a case study at accredited programs. I believe that I could use my story for good to help maybe inspire other people to find strength. The more meetings I had with the Social Work department, the clearer my decision became. I was beyond excited for my future.

As admirable as all of this sounds, I have to reign it back in and tell you about freshman year. It was a complete shit show. Not only did

I barely pass any of my classes, I drank, smoked, and did other college-like things on a massive level.

Party Brittany raged. Freedom was beautiful to me, and I abused it badly. I remember I got so drunk one night I got lost *on campus.* I was on campus and didn't know where I was. One of my best friends had to hijack a Domino's Pizza delivery car to come find me and bring me back to the dorm. I woke up under bushes off campus and in random other places. I greatly abused my past as a crutch to act like a complete reckless party animal. That feeling of comfort that I got from alcohol was unlike any other, just like in high school. When I was drunk and high, I didn't feel pain or like a black sheep or like I was struggling to fit in. I felt at ease. I felt as though being myself was good enough.

It was a slippery slope that could have gotten me killed or worse countless times. I didn't know when to stop drinking, so my body would stop for me in the form of blacking out. Most times I drank, it was to the point of blackout. I justified it by being a freshman in college. Everyone was doing it! In all reality, I was just being an asshole. It didn't matter what day of the week it was or if I had tests the following day. If there was a party, I was there (*Sorry, Aunt Val*).

Outside of drinking and nearly falling out first semester, I joined the modern dance company. I loved dance so much. I made friends with such amazing girls and it made me feel like I was a part of something amazing again, just like cheerleading in high school did. I ended up taking dance classes later on in college and fell in love with being on stage. I had wished that I was a better dancer like some of the girls who had been dancing their whole lives, but I was just thankful to be a part of it.

Meanwhile back at home, Mom had been saving up her disability checks in order for her to make the return to Florida. My grandmother and I tried to talk her out of it and asked her where she would go when she got there. She had nowhere to stay and everyone's funds were tapped to help her. She had no income plan. Nothing. But there was no stopping her. She was stubborn and determined to go "home" where she belonged. She hated the northeast. She hated the cold winter and the snow. She longed for sunshine and ocean waters. There was no stopping her. She purchased her Greyhound bus ticket, removed every last bit of evidence that she was ever living at my grandparents' home, and requested to be taken to the station.

I drove Mom and Grandma to Scranton Greyhound Bus Station one cold morning in January of 2008. Mom was so excited and talked about all of the things she was going to do when she got there. She told me she was going to get hot Krispy Kreme donuts just for me. She promised she would call and write often. I felt numb on the way there. I didn't know what to think. I was worried sick. I could tell Grandma was broken hearted, but she wanted her daughter to be happy.

We waited for Mom's bus to come. I took one last picture of us together and said goodbye. She smiled and waved and said she loved us. We watched the bus disappear and held each other and cried the whole way home. I knew that would be the last time I saw my mother.

I went back to school and got through freshman year. My grades left much to be desired, but I passed and went on to sophomore year. I felt like a true champion at life.

Summer 2008 was one of my favorite summers. I hung out with all of my friends from high school, and together we raised some serious hell. Again, I don't know how I lived through the drinking. I continued to be stupid and reckless and took advantage of mostly everything I had going for me. I used to justify it as, "This is what everyone does at my age!" But, in all reality, I had been through entirely too much to not know any better.

CHAPTER 16

After Mom left, we heard from her quite frequently for a while. Then letters and phone calls became further and further apart. Eventually we stopped hearing from her altogether. Grandma made Mom a promise before she left that no matter what happened, she would not look for her. She would not try to find her if she didn't want to be found. Grandma promised and never went back on her word, but as we stopped hearing from her, she contacted a private detective to see if there was any way to find out where she was without her knowing. She was worried sick. Personally, I tried not to think about it.

I went back to school the week before classes were going to begin my sophomore year. I was so excited to have an apartment off campus. I was moving in with two of my best friends from high school, and we were getting a third roommate that we didn't know.

There was a big block party across campus that Saturday night and everyone was going to celebrate being back. I remember exactly what I had to drink that night: two Rolling Rock beers, one shot of SKY Vodka, and a cup of "Jungle Juice" (*Jungle Juice was any kind of clear, cheap liquor poured into a giant cooler and mixed with gallons of Hawaiian Punch*). I was having a great time with my friends and catching up with everyone.

I sat outside to smoke a cigarette on the stoop and suddenly it got really quiet. I looked behind me and the lights were off and the door was shut. It's like I missed something. I turned around to a flashlight in my face. It was the Lock Haven Police. I was officially caught underage drinking. That same night, I lost my phone and it got ran over (*what a joy that evening was!*). I was taken back to my apartment in the police car and was told to be careful. I was given a fine and was told my license would be suspended.

"I am so dead! Dad is going to kill me. OMG!" So much panic and anxiety. I didn't think it was fair that I was the only one who got caught while there was an entire house full of people who were also drinking underage behind me. I didn't rat any of them out, of course, but I was pissed. The school year hadn't even started yet - good grief! Well, I knew I had to go home that weekend and break the news to Dad in person. This was going to be really bad.

The entire way home I rehearsed what I was going to say. When I finally reached the driveway, I felt ready to tell him what a real disappointment his daughter was.

I pulled into the driveway and saw Dad was mowing the lawn. I waved at him and sheepishly went into the house. I paced back and forth trying to make sense of what was about to happen and continued to internally beat myself up over it.

Then, the phone rang.

It was my grandma's number that came across the caller ID. I thought that was strange. Why would Grandma be calling Dad? She knows I'm at school. I answered the phone and it was the voice of my Uncle Rich. That seemed even more peculiar.

He said, "Hi, is Dan Cooley there? This is Rich Wilson."

I was too dumbfounded to even ask what was going on. I said, "Hi Uncle Rich. It's me, Brittany."

His voice changed and I could tell there was something really wrong. He said: "Oh, Hi Brittany. You're home. Uhhh...your grandma just got back from vacation with us and...you should come see her."

I knew something really bad must have happened. For my uncle to call and ask for my father when I am not supposed to be home and then turn the story around to invite me to come see grandma? Something happened to Mom. I just knew it.

I ran out of that house so fast, jumped in my car, turned the ignition, and flew down the driveway only to back up and tell Dad I was going to Grandma's and that I thought something was wrong with Mom. He said, "Okay honey, I love you."

A huge lump in my throat formed when I was pulling up in my grandma's driveway. I didn't want to know what was about to happen. I didn't want to know why Uncle Rich was calling Dad. I wanted to do anything and everything to turn around and drive away and pretend like whatever was about to happen wasn't happening.

I saw my grandmother holding her head in her hands in the grove where we spent many afternoons playing in my childhood. My uncle was standing next to her with a look of stone on his face. I got out of my car and approached my family. The rest was a blur.

I collapsed into my uncle. He held me up so I wouldn't fall to the ground. I was hyperventilating. I think. I don't know that I cried any actual tears. I couldn't process what was happening. It happened so fast.

"I'm sorry Brittany, but your Mom…." I don't remember if he said "died," "passed away," or "she's dead"… I can't remember the exact verbiage because I already knew the end of his sentence.

I sat with my grandmother. My aunt arrived soon after. Time stopped that day. We all sat in the grove together until dark.

The next week was blurry. Lots of calls and condolences. More food was brought to Grandma's than anyone could ever actually eat. Although, the food was a blessing because no one felt like cooking.

Grandma had made arrangements for Mom's body to be brought home to Pennsylvania. I made dozens of calls to the hospital trying to locate the nursing staff and doctor who had treated her to figure out what the hell happened. It didn't matter. I knew what had happened. She was destitute and malnourished and her body gave out. She had gone home to be with her Lord.

After all these years of suffering from her internal demons, she was at peace. I left her and she didn't make it. It was just as I had said all along.

Grandma finally had gotten through to someone who could contact the physician via email due to the fact that he was on vacation for ten days. That same afternoon, she received a personal phone call explaining what had taken place.

Mom had been brought into Pensacola Baptist Hospital with a bleeding ulcer. It was cauterized and she was discharged. When asked about family, she told the nurses that she had a mother and daughter in Pennsylvania, but she did not want them to be contacted. Three days later she was brought in, unconscious, and internally hemorrhaging. She was in surgery for nearly six hours and given an entire body's worth of blood.

The weekend I had been arrested, she was on her deathbed. She was destitute and ill. Unmedicated and uncared for. The waves of guilt hit me all at once. While I was out being a college jackass, Mom was dying. After finally letting go to allow myself a chance at a normal life and to forget about our time in Florida, what I had been saying since I was 7 years old had become true: she wouldn't make it without me. I left her and she died.

Suddenly my pending license suspension, meeting with the Dean and my fine became completely irrelevant. I felt as though I was guilty of murder by abandonment.

I didn't spend enough time with her when I was home. I didn't tell her how much I loved her as much as I should have. I avoided her at all costs because she was so mentally ill. I couldn't bear to have a conversation with her. I couldn't look at her because she had reminded me of awful things. Suddenly, all of the tragedy that we had faced together didn't matter. Suddenly, I didn't remember how sick she was or her delusional ways of thinking.

I remembered Super Mom.

I remembered Linda Sue Wilson Cooley, the Executive Director of a successful non-profit organization. The mom who sprinkled glitter on my pillow from the Tooth Fairy, the one who spent thousands of dollars on Disney collector's plates and displayed them in my playroom, who swung me around in our living room, ho sang like the angels and whose smile lit up the entire world. I remembered the courageous pillar of strength who gave me life. And now she was dead.

Her entire life she struggled. From childhood until her last breath, she fought to survive. She had only a few short years of true happiness before her demons robbed her and took it all away. My heart broke for the life she lived and the life that was taken from her. I took responsibility. I wished so badly that I could have spent another day with her to make sure she knew how much I loved her.

To this day, I truly believe that she died thinking I didn't love her. I'll never ever forgive myself for that.

I picked out the outfit that she was buried in. It was a beachy outfit, capri pants and a sleeveless flowy tank, something I could see her wearing while walking along the sandy white beaches of Pensacola. I picked out her casket. It was a beautiful seafoam green. It reminded me of the waters in the Gulf of Mexico that she loved so much. I picked out her headstone, rose quartz. She couldn't just have a regular grey color. It was too generic for her.

I called the pallbearers that Grandma and I had chosen to ask and requested their presence. All of the men I asked said yes without hesitation. I requested that Moonlight Sonata be played. It was her favorite to play on the piano, and I had even learned how to play the first few lines when i was little so I could be just like her.

Oh, how I wished I could go back to playing the piano with my mom.

Her funeral was beautiful. So many people showed up that we didn't expect. A lot of my friends from high school and college came to support me. I was so grateful to be surrounded with love and support, but it didn't make the guilt or sense of responsibility for my Mom being in that closed casket go away. I wasn't able to see her to say goodbye.

The funeral director had told us that her body had decomposed entirely too much to be seen in an open casket. I was angry that she wasn't put on ice to be preserved through transport, but it was for the best that her withering body wasn't my last memory of her.

I kept my shit together through the service as best I could. Seeing Dad so upset as he came through the receiving line is when I broke the first time. I saw how much his heart was hurting in his eyes. This time, it wasn't my fault, but I still felt as though it was. Despite everything Mom had put him through, he had loved her more than anything in the whole world. My father is a man of few words and rarely shows emotion, but that day he cried with me. He held me up in the line and said how much he loved me (*She left him in the divorce. I'll never understand why. Maybe my life would have turned out differently if she had never done that*).

Grandma gave a beautiful eulogy. I was so amazed that she had such strength to do that. She had more strength than me. I couldn't. I didn't say anything at all. I had written a passage to be read by my cousin JoAnne. I really lost it when my cousin, Brian, got up to say something and turned to me on the podium to say, "I want to tell Brittany about her mom."

That was the most painful, to have everyone's eyes on me. Looks of sympathy and grief all directed at me. It just made my guilt worse. Brian grew up with Mom and had so many stories about their childhood together. I loved to imagine her as a young vibrant child full of life. I had wished that had been her whole life.

My sister came too. She was my life-saving grace. I wouldn't have made it from the church to the cemetery in one conscious piece without her. Although I didn't grow up with her like I had wanted to, she was *always* there when I needed her the most. If one person would show, it was Jaime.

I rode in her jeep to the cemetery and sucked down nearly ten cigarettes on the approximately six mile ride. I didn't even care if anyone saw me. I hid my habit from my whole family and worked hard to do so. That day, I didn't care.

The time at the cemetery was mostly a blur. Grandma's pastor spoke again. The casket was placed over the hole that had been dug for her final resting place. I remember seeing Grandma sobbing and gave the casket one final tap as she walked away. I think I cried all the tears I had back in the church. I held on to my dad and my sister, Jaime on one side and Dad on the other.

That was one of the hardest days of my life. I wanted to put it behind me the best way I knew how: lock it in a box deep inside of me and forget about it. It's what I had done my whole life with every feeling I had ever faced. So, two weeks since the news of Mom passing away, I went back to school to finish out my sophomore year. Everyone told me to take a semester off and really take all the time I needed. Even the Dean of Student Affairs thought it was a good idea when we spoke at our meeting about my underage-drinking citation. Surprisingly, she didn't care and didn't make me pay the school fine. I showed her my mother's obituary and she teared up and said, "You just go home and be with your family. Just make sure your name never comes across my desk again."

I plunged back into school head first. I absolutely had to become the best social worker and save kids' lives. That was the only way that all of this would be made right. I couldn't save Mom, so I had to get my degree in order to save a bunch of kids like me. I felt it in my soul. It was more than a career, it was a purpose. I was going to get all of the little Brittany's out there to safety and justice to preserve their childhood and innocence. That was the only way I could suppress the grief and guilt that lingered within my soul.

CHAPTER 16

I made it through college just as I had through high school. I graduated with my Bachelor's degree in Social Work on May 6, 2011 from Lock Haven University of Pennsylvania. On time. It was another incredibly monumental day in my life. I didn't graduate with any fancy ropes attached to my robe, but I graduated. I even made the Dean's List the last two semesters and my Dad was so proud he still has the certificate hanging on his refrigerator to this day.

I was full of dreams and ideas after graduation. I couldn't believe that I had made it. I, Brittany Cooley, was a true warrior and made no excuses. Aunt Val said a diploma was non-negotiable, and I made it happen.

After graduation I moved out to Meadville, Pennsylvania with my boyfriend of two years. His parents owned a campground and offered me a summer job while I searched for one within my field. I had a great summer but knew I didn't want to stay there. I wanted to move home to be closer to my family. In November of 2011, we moved across the state back to my tiny town in hopes to begin a life together.

I got my first job working with adults while I completed the process of taking the civil service exam and waiting for a position to open up in Child Protective Services. Overall, life was good. I had my first job in the field and my own apartment with my serious boyfriend. All stars were aligning in my favor. Little did I know things were about to get incredibly fucking complicated.

In February of 2012, I received a letter with an interview request for Bradford County Pennsylvania for the Department of Human Services, Children and Youth. I was so excited for a job that literally zero people want to do. I wanted to be the best CYS Caseworker there was. I wanted to work my way up to CPS Investigator and embrace my inner badass. Maybe I would even go to the police academy to be a cop! I wanted to be more than a hero. I wanted to make up for all of the mistakes I had made and make a difference in kids' lives. I wanted to put families back together and remove children from the neglect and abuse. I wanted to be the person that I needed way back then.

I thought of my caseworker, Shannon, and hoped that she would be proud of me. I often wished I could contact her and let her know I turned out alright and that she inspired me to literally grow up and be like her. It was a total dream come true. I was excited to become the super hero that I was destined to be. I scheduled the interview and pretty much was guaranteed the job. This was it. I did it.

In the midst of all of this job excitement, another part of me was brought to light. Before I get into this, I want you to know that my perspective on relationships and intimacy isn't "normal." I know that. My childhood shaped much of who I am today. I am a survivor on many fronts. However, that week my innocence was stolen when I was 13 completely shut off my ability to express emotions in a physical way. I had no sense of sacred feels when it came to sex. It's not special. It's just sex. Always.

When you experience any kind of sexual trauma, especially as a child, there are two extremes that I have studied among fellow victims: 1) you won't let anyone touch you or 2) you let everyone touch you. I was the latter. Now, before you start slut shaming me, let me explain. I do not put myself in the "slut" category. Do I regret a few college nights? Are there several people I wish I could magic erase off my "list?" DEFINITELY. I don't feel poorly about admitting that either. The point I am trying to make here, is that sex isn't sacred. It's just an act. To me, anyway.

Having sex was just like brushing my teeth, putting on deodorant, or taking a shower. It was just another thing that you had to do, a regular part of life. There was no magic or butterflies or tender moments like I had watched on TV or even heard my friends discuss. That was all foreign to me. Sex was expected and not respected. I remember having a conversation with a college friend who was talking about buying a special outfit for her first time. I remember blurting, "Ugh what for? Don't you just want to get it over with?" Because I did. Every time.

I never had any of those kinds of feelings. I could say with 100% confidence that I could live without it. My friends would look at me in horror. I would laugh, because I literally could not comprehend what they described as sex. I never related it to my abuse. I never even thought about it like that. I just didn't have any attachment to any kind of...extracurricular activities. I'd rather go without ANY day. The point of having sex is reaching the 'O' and I could do that by myself. So really, I wouldn't be missing anything.

I loved love. I loved the idea of being in love. I loved the romantic gestures and all of the Valentine's Day bullshit, but outside of that, love was hollow. I was content in my relationship. I had worked hard to get where I wanted to be with my boyfriend. I had to work really hard for him to even give me a chance. I truly loved him. He moved across the state away from everything he had ever known for Christ's sake! He was in this with me. He also got offered a position within Child Protective Services soon after I did. It was a nearly perfect pairing.

Until I met her.

CHAPTER 17

One night I was out with my boyfriend downtown at a smoke-filled dive bar, and she was there. Her smile lit up the room and her laugh just made you smile too. Girls are notorious for using the buddy system, so after five beers we were both due for a bathroom break.

I was looking in the mirror waiting my turn and made some kind of negative statement about myself. I look fat, I am fat... I don't remember. It doesn't matter, it's all the same gist. I didn't have very good self-esteem and saw my value in what others thought of me. People pleasing was what I did best to survive, particularly in social situations.

She grabbed my shoulders, spun me around, and took my face in both of her hands. She firmly but softly kissed me on the lips. Before I could even process what was happening, she pulled away and said, "Don't ever call yourself that again." I had been drinking so I chalked it up to the booze initially, but I felt something that night that I had never felt in my entire life. I felt passion. I felt sacred. I felt whatever that feeling is that you feel when your crush asks you out. My face grew hot and I thought I was going to pass out. Then panic set in and I rushed out of the bathroom and went back to the bar to be with my boyfriend.

Holy shit. What the fuck just happened? My poor boyfriend was sitting out at the bar waiting for me. One innocent, tipsy trip to the bathroom and BOOM. Life changed forever. The thing is, I didn't feel guilty about it. Like, at all. I didn't see it as information I had to share with him and I didn't see it as cheating. She was a girl. It totally didn't count. Right?

Wrong.

The next day she texted me and asked me if I thought she was weird or if I regretted it. I said no. But, I made sure to tell her that I wasn't gay and that it would never happen again. She also had a boyfriend so it was wrong on all fronts.

I had an internal conversation with myself. "Brittany, you are not gay. You have a boyfriend. You were just two drunk girls in a bathroom. It was nothing to feel guilty over. It meant nothing. Next time, cool it on the beer. Don't go to bars she's at. She's bad news." I almost felt guilty that I didn't feel guiltier. Because I didn't. Honestly, I wanted it to happen again. It was like a dirty exciting little secret. But, I could never admit that. Until, our dirty exciting little secret went out the window.

Our friendship continued on and we grew closer as time went by. We became even more inseparable. Many more kisses and messages happened that made me feel some kind of alive that I had never felt before. We would make random trips to the grocery store just to spend some time together. I was living a double life. It became insane. I was living a big lie.

I felt like a terrible person. The guilt I finally started to feel was nearly suffocating at times. But the feeling that I had when I was with her overruled it every time. I knew what I was doing was wrong. I knew that it would hurt him badly if he ever found out. I swore he never would.

Until he did.

I was put on 'probation' and he had control of my phone and all of my passwords to everything. He didn't want me going anywhere or seeing her ever again. I was beyond distraught, but I knew he was right. I couldn't realistically be with her. I could never tell my family. There was no future for us.

I told her that I couldn't hang out with her anymore and that I was sorry. It nearly killed me to send those messages. I went into a deep depression after breaking things off with her. But, honestly, what were we thinking? We were literally crazy. I had to reality check myself and prioritize my life. Starting with my boyfriend and work.

Meanwhile back at my dream job, I was drowning. I was drowning in paperwork and phone calls. I was given an incredibly difficult case and it drained the living shit out of me. The only thing that gave me any kind of relief was her, and she was gone now. I realized I couldn't live without her, so I worked out a way that we could be friends. I would rather be her friend with strict boundaries than lose her completely. We would go for walks every night together because she lived only two blocks up the road. We even hung out as couples. It was good to be friends.

But it wasn't good enough.

June came around and I decided I needed some time apart from my boyfriend. I wasn't happy and was incredibly confused, so I asked or a break. I needed space. She and I planned a getaway to the beach.

We spent three days at the Jersey Shore together. We were even in the background of the TV show as they were filming the last season. We ate the best food and drank strong drinks and forgot all of our problems that awaited us at home.

I fell in love with her that weekend. If I hadn't already, I knew it in my bones. One weekend wasn't long enough. I wished we could run away together forever and start over. I didn't ever want to leave. I knew what was coming when I returned home. I knew I would have to face the reality that we were star-crossed and there was no future.

CHAPTER 18

When I returned to reality, there was a crippling heaviness in my body. It felt worse than anything I can describe to you in words. I felt as though I was living in a prison. I could be outside and still feel so trapped. I was incredibly depressed. My thoughts grew morbid and I just put myself on autopilot and went about my life.

I said goodbye to my lover and told her we could no longer see each other for good. It was wrong, and I had to be with my boyfriend because that is what I was 'supposed' to do. I remember one night she stood outside my window and demanded that I come down. I turned her away and shattered both her and me into a thousand pieces. It was one of the hardest decisions I've ever made.

It felt as though everyone needed more of me than I had to give. My anxiety ate me alive so badly that I went to the emergency room twice in a full blown panic attack, begging for relief. Not once was I asked if I had thoughts of hurting myself. If I had been asked that question, I would have likely said yes. Work continued to pile up. The more it piled, the less I cared.

I began to lose all will to live and grew a stronger passion for death. I began to fantasize about being in a terrible car accident or being in the wrong place at the wrong time and being killed. I wished there was a way out.

I stopped going to work. I just didn't go. I made some bullshit excuses that I was sick, but I was at the point of having a nervous breakdown. I couldn't take care of anyone. Hell, I couldn't even take care of myself.

During this time, my boyfriend and I still lived together but we may as well not have been together. My emotional state took a significant toll on him too. It's as if he took on some of my pain and he did not know how to process it either. He would do his best to encourage me to get out of bed and do even the most basic of tasks, but I would adamantly refuse. I was slipping farther and farther away from him as I isolated myself from everything and everyone. He likely felt like he was making it worse and stopped trying to reach out. I can't say that I noticed in the moment because I already felt so alone, but I see his hopelessness in hindsight.

For the first time in my life, after all of the problems I had fixed, obstacles I had hurdled, impossible situations I made possible, I really saw no way out. There was no hope. There really was no light at the end of the tunnel. I was stuck in a life I had worked so hard to create for myself and I hated every ounce of it. I felt damaged and suffocated. On the outside it looked like I had everything together, but on the inside I wanted nothing more than to go to sleep and not wake up.

The emergency room prescribed me anti-anxiety medicine that I ate like candy just to survive the waking moments of my day. I took more than prescribed just to keep me out of a conscious state because I couldn't handle it.

I was paralyzed by fear of disappointment and failure. My mind raced with worst case scenarios. When I was awake, I was crying and shaking uncontrollably in a corner of my bed. My entire world was crumbling and there was nothing I could do about it. I didn't have answers. I had no rational ideas or thoughts. I was broken, and I couldn't put myself back together. I felt as though I had no control over anything.

This lasted for five straight days. My entire life was a struggle. I failed at the most important things I had been given. I failed my mom, my calling, my boyfriend, and hurt an innocent beautiful person in the process. There was truly no way out of this.

Out of seemingly nowhere, a wave of relief washed over me. I gained clarity. I found peace. I realized I had control over what was happening to me. After all, I created it. I knew exactly what I had to do to stop it. I was about to solve my problems in a way that I'd neglected to all along: I knew it was my time to bow out.

For the first time in over a week, I left the apartment. I went to the Dandy Mini Mart in Towanda and purchased myself a drink and some food. I hadn't eaten in days. I saw one of my coworkers there. She asked how I was doing. I remember telling her that everything was going to be fine and I was feeling much better. I made sure I told her how much I looked up to her. She was one badass investigator. She was everything I wanted to become. Sadly, I would never get that chance because I just wasn't cut out for it. I was sad that I had failed but incredibly grateful that this nightmare was almost over.

On July 17th, 2012 I woke up. I kissed my boyfriend goodbye as he went to work. I told him I would need another day to get back to the office. He was concerned, but left anyway. I don't blame him. I had been very convincing and he had a career to build. I couldn't stand in his way anymore. I had hurt him enough. He had given up and sacrificed the world to be with me. He loved me so much and even took me back after the affair I had with another woman. I truly loved him so much and was so happy I was about to do him a huge favor. After all, I didn't deserve him. I did not deserve anyone. I was ready to go see my mama.

I wrote a note. It read: *"I am sorry for the mess I have made. Please forgive me and find peace. It is my time to go be with my mom. I love you and I will always be with you."*

I read it over and over. I decided that it was too dramatic and this would not be an unexpected event. My life had been a roller coaster. It was currently a *mess*. I didn't need to leave a note or explanation. This was obviously inevitable. I ripped it up and threw it into the trashcan in the kitchen.

I retrieved a ceramic knife with a blue handle from the silverware drawer. I paced the kitchen for what seemed like an hour. I walked into the living room area with the blade tightly pressed against my stomach. I took a deep breath, I prayed, and I plunged it into my belly.

Panic set it. I hadn't done research. What if I didn't hit something that would bleed out fast enough? I felt nothing, but the blood began to pool around me as I hit the floor. I don't know if I passed out due to seeing my own blood or if it was the actual blood loss. Either way, it was the last thing I remember before hearing the police department bust in the door.

I was placed on a stretcher and taken down the stairs to be loaded into the back of an ambulance. The EMT's tried to keep me awake. I remember the sirens being so loud inside of the vehicle. I was patiently waiting for the lights to go out, to peacefully go into the darkness and find my mom. This was happening all wrong.

I was wheeled into the emergency room upon arrival to the Robert Packer Hospital in Sayre, Pennsylvania. They began to cut my clothes off of my body and prepare me for surgery. A team of doctors hovered over my body, blocking out the blinding fluorescent lights. A man leaned in close to my face with a surgical mask on and he asked me, "Sweetheart, is there anyone that we can call for you?"

In the midst of all of my internal turmoil, I never once thought of my dad. To be left alone in complete heartache. I envisioned the hot tears rolling down his cheek as he received the news. I never considered what it would be like for him to bury his daughter next to his late ex-wife. While I was doing everything I could to make it through the day, I never thought about how my decision to end my suffering would affect the most important person on the planet. If anything was worth living for, he was.

That was my light bulb moment. A huge rush of adrenaline and reality backhanded me right in the soul and I cried out, "My Dad! Oh my God, my Dad!!" He didn't deserve to get this phone call. He did not deserve this pain. I begged the doctors to call my dad and tell him that I was so sorry. I begged them to save my life so I could spend the rest of it making this up to him.

Then a mask was placed over my face and everything went black.

CHAPTER 19

I woke up around 3:00 AM in the worst physical pain of my life. It was dark. I was alone. I could hear the beep of monitors surrounding me. I had tubes coming out of every hole in my body. There were a total of 26 staples in my stomach. I was alive.

I realized that I was alone. I realized that there was no one coming to save me from the turmoil that surrounded my life and got me to this very point. I realized I had to save myself. Despite my physical pain, I realized I had the power to save myself. I pledged to myself in that moment that I was going to do whatever it took to create a beautiful life that I loved to live so I would never end up in this dark ICU ever again.

I realized I lived because there was some purpose to my life and I was going to do my best to figure out exactly what that was.

The next few days were painful, both physically and mentally. I had dozens of visitors that showed up to express their love and support. My entire family came and sat with me. They took turns. I was showered with flowers and gifts. Seeing my dad for the first time afterwards was the hardest visit. I saw his all-too-familiar expression of absolute heartbreak on his face. He looked at me like I was a broken little doll and he had no idea where the glue was to fix me. I vowed to myself that I would never see that expression on his face again. I knew I had *a lot* of work to do and a long road ahead.

I was okay with that.

I was moved from the ICU to a regular room until I had physically recovered enough to have the epidural taken out of my back and all of the tubes removed. My sister came from Delaware and stayed with me. She was my watchdog and caretaker. She braided my hair, helped bathe me, and got rid of any unwanted company. We didn't grow up together and at the time we weren't really that close, but she was always showed up when I needed her. She dropped everything and came to my side. I was more than grateful.

Then came the hardest part. The part that I did not predict. The worst part of this entire experience: my transfer to the psychiatric unit with an indefinite sentence. I had to be thankful I wasn't in the morgue, but I wasn't sure if this was going to be a better alternative. I wasn't sure how I was going to survive it.

I begged my dad not to let them take me. I didn't belong in there. I wasn't crazy. I was *not* my mother! As the security guard wheeled me to the locked elevator, Dad looked at me and said, "I think you better go and get better honey. I love you." I had never cried so hard in my life.

How did I get here? This actual place? The same place I visited my mother and ran out of when we had poor visits. The same place I had clients and visited them. This time, I had no access to leave. I had a wristband, an all access pass to the locked unit for the severest of mental illnesses. I was a patient. If I had thought my life was a nightmare before, I had no idea what to call this. It was a terrible realization to see myself come full circle to this moment, where my mother used to be. It was like I was being locked away and the key was being thrown out. There was no way to prepare for this.

They wheeled me off the elevator. I had to sit and wait for the nurses to check me in. I was in nothing but a hospital gown. I had never felt so humbled. When I was processed and given a room assignment, I asked if I was able to shower. They said of course, but I was not allowed any kind of soap and, of course, no razors. I could only use what was provided. The only difference from jail was that I didn't have to shower in front of others.

I sat in my room and cried. I was alone and locked away. I had no idea how I was going to make it out of this place. I had no idea where I was going to go from here. I had no plan. I just knew that I was alive and this was my fault. I put myself here, but how was I supposed to find the strength to get out and live a normal life again? Where would I work? What would I do? Now that I had this stigma attached to me, I didn't feel as though it would be possible for me to lead a normal life. I felt like people could see it written all over me, like a brand on my skin.

I had to come to terms with the fact that I was broken and I needed fixing. I had 26 staples holding my stomach together to remind me of that. As if I could forget. Maybe there really was no hope for me.

Maybe I was destined to be a ward of the state, taken care of for the rest of my life in a place like this. That would be easy. I thought about not having to hold any responsibility for anything, having everything handled for me, living off of the government like Mom did because she was too ill to work. Was I really incapable of being a functioning member of society? Was I really so incapable of managing life and things like a stressful career and relationship problems? Would anyone ever want or trust me again? Why did I fucking care so much? All of these questions circled my head as my Clonazepam kicked in and I drifted off to sleep.

The next day I was woken up at 6 AM for meds and given my schedule for the day. I wanted no part of the group activities. I just wanted to isolate. But I knew that if I didn't behave, I wouldn't be able to have visitors and I would never get out of there. I remember the doctor saying he did not see me being discharged anytime soon. As far as he was concerned, I was sentenced to life and going to have to work to be paroled on good behavior.

I changed my attitude on the third day because something finally came over me to push me to get my shit together. I had the realization that I did not come this far to only come this far. I realized that life is really what you make of it, and I was about to waste the precious second chance I was given. I came to terms that I really deserved to be in that locked unit. Not just for me, but for my family's peace of mind.

I put my head down and made the best of the experience because I was alive. And *that* was the most amazing thing I had going for me.

I was in the locked unit for six days and discharged under the conditions that I would complete two full weeks of outpatient intensive therapy and attend all of my follow up appointments. I was given the diagnosis of Major Depressive Disorder and put on a colorful cocktail of medications.

I was released and my dad picked me up in his brand new 2012 GT Mustang. I was free. I had a lot of work to do, but I was ready for it all.

I realized that being myself was the best thing I could be. It really didn't matter what anyone thought. I couldn't afford to care what anyone thought of me anymore. I knew I deserved to be happy. Even if no one else understood it. I took it day by day, hour by hour, and slowly began to pick up the pieces and put together a beautiful life. I embraced the courage I needed to make the necessary changes to be truly happy.

I broke up with my boyfriend and moved in with my girlfriend. We lived a happy life together for nearly four years. We went our separate ways, but I can assure you that I have no regrets, only amazing memories. She was one of the best things that had ever happened to me. She gave me the courage to be who I am and taught me so much about myself.

I also quit my job at Children and Youth Services. It was the root of the majority of my anxiety at the time. I spent nearly six years working in adult mental health. I helped individuals who suffered from severe mental illness rebuild their life post psychiatric hospitalization. I let go of what I thought was my calling and instead embraced my purpose.

In 2014, I joined a network marketing business that gave me the taste of entrepreneurship and freedom. I became wildly obsessed with working for myself and saying goodbye to the dreaded nine to five. I learned the ropes of social media marketing and built a platform for myself where I shared a brief version of this story for the very first time. I had no intentions of ever sharing it with anyone. I had planned on creating a new identity and pretending like my past never happened.

I had the realization after I had purchased brittanycooley.com and shared my story of tragedy to triumph, that it wasn't about me at all. It was about who needed to hear my message of hope. If I had read this book in the spring of 2012, it would have prevented me from making that huge mistake. I chose to become the person that I needed when I was internally suffering. I built who I am today on the ruins of my rock bottom moments. Defeat was never in my cards. Even when I tried to defeat myself.

In 2017, I began my very own company, Branding by Britt. I had become consumed by the power of sharing my journey and connecting with hundreds of people on social media. I had found that who I was and have come to be was much more important than any product or service I could provide.

Successful businesses are built on human connection. I was quick to catch onto this concept and discovered the power of my voice attached to a selfie, rather than a generic post. I labeled myself a Social Media Branding Coach with a specialty in Instagram. I knew that I could be of help to someone struggling as an online entrepreneur. I knew my methods were better than any generic shit any company taught. I believed it with all my soul. That showed through thankfully and allowed me to have a four-figure launch.

Since then, I have had the pleasure of traveling and working with over 300 online entrepreneurs to help them define their brand and be confidently, unapologetically themselves. Because being yourself is the best branding and value you have to offer anyone.

I am often asked what motivates me. There are a lot of things that motivate me truthfully, I am inspired by everyone in some way, shape, or form. Ultimately, there are three very important individuals who I owe my success to. On the days when I have wanted to throw in the towel or the battles have seemed too great, the following three people have lifted me up to repeatedly rise from the ashes.

First, Aunt Val. Her voice is always in the back of my head with every decision I make. I have an imaginary W.W.A.V.D. (What would Aunt Val do?) bracelet on at all times. Although, I don't always do what she would do, I like to take her opinion into consideration because it is always worth its weight in gold. She pushed me to be better and to do better, and therefore I *was* better. I never had a victim mentality and I owe that to her. I am so grateful that she treated me as one of her own. I can honestly say that I feel as though I can stand proud next to her children and, although I am no scholar and still no athlete, I am equal.

Second, I am here to put my best foot forward every day for my dad. That man is a pillar of strength and is forever my hero. I wouldn't have made it here without him. I take credit for every grey hair on his head. I can't imagine how hard the past 29 years have been being my parent.

Last but most certainly not least, my mom. Though I knew her longer as a monster, I choose to remember her as Super Mom and honor her memory as a woman full of life and joy that was overtaken against her will. I am here to create a beautiful life for myself that my mom would have loved to live alongside me. I keep her in my heart every moment and know she is with me. My heart will eternally break for the difficult, beaten path that she lived. I often dream of her smiling and laughing, swinging me around in circles in our living room.

CHAPTER 20

Even after all of this time, I still struggle with a scarcity mindset. Little hungry Brittany who washes her hair in the sink at Barnes and Noble and wants to protect her mom still lingers. Some things affect me more than others. Mother's Day is one of the hardest days of the year because it is an annual reminder of what was stolen from me. I am unable to use ceramic knives. I have night terrors. I am terrible at being in a committed relationship because I feel confined by the attachment and refuse to settle. I don't feel as though I am anchored or belong in any one place. I always feel that I am just passing through.

I will never forgive myself for putting my loved ones though the nightmare that I did when I tried to take my own life. I will never forget the look on my father's face when I saw him for the first time after my attempt. It is burned into my memory forever. I work hard every day to make sure that I will never see that expression on anyone's face ever again, particularly his. So, I have chosen hope.

I have worked hard to overcome my demons. I've learned not to dwell on the things I cannot change and focus on the things that I can. I can't change the mistakes I have made, but I can share them with you in hopes to inspire you not to make the same ones. Or, if you already have, I hope to inspire you to look at them as learning opportunities to grow from. To see the silver lining in even the darkest of days.

Despite any of my past, my future is bright and full. I am excited to travel the world, make enough money to take care of my entire family for life, fall in love, and create thousands of happy moments for the rest of my days. It will happen because I choose to make it so.

This life is what you create it to be. You have everything within you to have everything you have ever wanted. If you have a vision, you have the vessel. Life doesn't happen to you, it happens *for* you. And you're stronger because of it. Remember that needing and asking for help is not a weakness, it is a strength.

Your story surely isn't over yet. There is always hope if you look hard enough and choose to see it. Know that no matter what you've been through, it is in your control to make your life and circumstances better. Know that sometimes things may get worse first. Know that your dreams matter and you have a purpose that only you can fulfill in this world. You may not want to believe that, but I am living proof of purpose through pain. Your pain has purpose too.

If I can inspire you to do anything in this life, it is to go out and live your best life with zero regrets. Love every second of the life that you have been given. Be UNAPOLOGETIC AS FUCK and confident in who you are.

Unless you can choose to be a unicorn. Then you should always choose to be a unicorn.

Thank you from the bottom of my heart for taking the time to read my story. I ask that you share this book with a friend, loved one, or someone you feel it may impact.

If you or someone you know is struggling with thoughts of suicide, call the National Suicide Hotline: 1-800-273-8255

Instagram: @TheBrittanyCooley
Facebook: FB.com/brittcool
www.BrittanyCooley.com